From Cle[illegible] Castles: A St Kildan Looks Back

The Autobiography of

Calum MacDonald

The Islands Book Trust

First published in 2010 by The Islands Book Trust
Reprinted 2020

www.theislandsbooktrust.com

ISBN: 978-0-9560764-6-5

British Library Cataloguing in Publication Data. A CIP record for this book can be obtained from the British Library.

The Islands Book Trust would like to thank John MacDonald, Alasdair MacEachen and Donnie Morrison for their help with the production of this volume.

The Islands Book Trust, Community Hub, Balallan,
Isle of Lewis HS2 9PN. Tel: 01851 830 316

Typeset by Erica Schwarz (www.schwarz-editorial.co.uk)
Printed by Martins the Printers, Berwick upon Tweed, TD15 1RS, UK

Contents

Foreword

It gives me great pleasure to introduce the latest Islands Book Trust publication, *From Cleits to Castles – The Autobiography of Calum MacDonald.*

I am delighted to see Calum's life story published in full for the first time. It is one of the very few accounts provided by a native St Kildan of life on the island.

On a personal note, St Kilda, the place and the history have aroused my interest and given me much to think about and enjoy since I first visited the archipelago in the early 1980s. Since then, I have undertaken many excursions out west, ranging from daytrips to several days or a week at a time ... there is just something about the place that keeps drawing one back time after time. I kept a tally at one time but lost count somewhere around the thirtieth trip!

I recall Michael Robson describing his first sight of St Kilda from the hills of Harris and at once feeling the desire to get there. That same feeling may indeed describe my own desire to get there thirty years ago as I looked out to St Kilda from my home on the north-west coast of Benbecula. I was born in Uist in the year the Royal Artillery Range commenced operations in the islands, and St Kilda featured prominently in the activity around us as we grew up alongside Army families. Army personnel moved between Benbecula and St Kilda and many of the local male workforce were employed by civilian contractors engaged in work on the Range and on St Kilda, as they are to this day, albeit in fewer numbers.

Although many accounts have been written about St Kilda and its history, new information, new photographs and stories continue to appear from a variety of sources. Over the years,

I have made many friends in St Kilda circles and I am always interested to meet people who have a St Kilda story to tell. In recent years I have been privileged to meet Neil Ferguson living in Maidens, Ayrshire; Nancy MacDonald in Fort William, and John MacDonald at his home in Kinsale, Co. Cork, Ireland, all of whom have strong links with St Kilda.

It was on one of my visits to Kinsale that John and I discussed the possibility of publishing his father's autobiography in full, and as the idea developed it was decided that the publication would be a fitting contribution to the celebration of the eightieth anniversary of the evacuation of St Kilda.

I am grateful to all who have helped bring this project to fruition: those who provided photographs, many of which have not been published before; the Islands Book Trust for taking care of the publishing, and especially John for his assistance and advice. It is a great privilege to have John with us to launch this remarkable record of his father's memories.

Alasdair MacEachen
Benbecula
Outer Hebrides
August 2010

That was 2010, and now ten years on, we are commemorating the 90th anniversary of the evacuation of St Kilda.

St Kilda remains, but the St Kildans have gone. Both Neil Ferguson and Nancy MacDonald mentioned above are no longer with us and as we treasure the memories of those in "A Far Better Place" to quote Calum MacDonald, we must now play our part in passing on the stories and knowledge of St Kilda and its people to future generations.

To mark their departure from the island on 29th August 1930, we are publishing a special edition of this popular title with the support and encouragement of members of the author's family.

Alasdair MacEachen
Chairman IBT
August 2020

Preface

What I am about to write may not be of any significance to today's population, living in a more modern society, although it may give an insight into another way of life.

This story spans sixty-eight years, from my early remembrances as a youth on Hirta, as St Kilda was called in my mother's Gaelic tongue, until yesterday, 30th March 1976 – the day of my retirement in the great City of London, where I have worked for the last twenty-six years as a valet in Grosvenor House, Park Lane. There I met many people of different creeds and cultures. Some I came to know as friends, whom I shall always remember as real fellow men. Many were rich and famous, two categories I never belonged to, simply because I was born poor, but nevertheless I have been happy by birth and by nature.

I was born in 1908, to a large family of eleven, of which eight are still alive today. The oldest living, my brother, is seventy-nine years old, and the youngest is my sister, who is fifty-six years old.

On the island there lived sixteen families, most of whom were closely related through intermarriage. My family tree dates back to 1753.

My great grandmother came from Lochinver, a Miss Betsy Scott, who was born in 1816. When she came to the island as a servant maid to the minister, she married my great grandfather whom I was christened after, 'Calum'. On the island we all lived by the same standards and education. Our English education was limited, as we only spoke in Gaelic most of the time. English was taught in a small school by the missionary's wife who was a Gaelic/English teacher. The missionary and his wife came from the mainland of Scotland, and although she was a qualified teacher, it was quite a task for her to teach us the English language. Therefore my basic English is limited as far as writing and speaking goes, yet no person throughout my life ever told me I was illiterate.

All my life I have been very fortunate because I was born among a small community of Christian belief, who lived and shared their lives as a whole, not as a unit. Our closeness was partly due to kinship and isolation from the outside world.

Calum MacDonald

Sixteen families, sixteen crofts and sixteen houses made up the main street on St Kilda (Alasdair MacEachen)

Chapter 1

Naturally no person remembers the day he was born, and neither do I. My uncle, though, who lived next door to us on Hirta, could remember that day very well and never let a chance slip by without reminding me of the fact. He was a thickset and powerful-looking man with black hair and a black beard which reached halfway down his chest. He was my mother's eldest brother. His own family numbered three sons and four daughters, so he knew all there was to know about childbirth. At the time I knew my uncle he was a widower. His moods were very changeable and he could be very cantankerous when he was in a bad mood. Our families were always in and out of each other's houses. My uncle was very fond of his pipe and his black twist tobacco and his chair by the fireplace. When I entered he would look at me with his piercing eyes and say, 'Every time you look down at your navel you will remember your old uncle, for it was me who cut your navel cord the day you were born, and don't you ever forget it. I suppose I should have twisted your little neck that day as you were wriggling and crying like a pussycat.' Of course I knew this was said in good humour at the revelation of my birth, as he was proud of the fact that he had been the midwife and had carried out the job successfully. He again reminded me of the fact thirty-three years on when he was a very old and lonely man. I will relate of this later on in my story.

When I asked my mother if what my uncle said was true, she said it was. Most of the villagers were up in the hills with only a couple of elderly women left behind at home. My mother did not feel too well and after mid-day she went to lie down on the bed for a while. Soon after, my mother started in labour and called to my sister Annie, who was eight years old, to go for help. Annie did not realise what was taking place as she ran out of the house and spotted Uncle Finlay in the field below. She ran to him and told him mother was ill and wanted help right away. When he got up to the house and into the bedroom he heard a baby's cry. He had never faced such an urgent situation in his life before. He rolled up his sleeves and told my sister to get hot water, then he took out his pocket knife, dipped it in the boiling water, and proceeded with the operation to sever the umbilical cord, knotting it at both ends; mother's and mine. The operation completed, he told my sister to go and inform one of the old women to come at once and finish the necessary part of nature, then he walked out of the room. Today I can look down and say, 'Well done, Uncle, you did a mighty good job, and I am sorry for any embarrassment I might have caused you, when coming into this world.'

My earliest recollection as a boy is a very happy one, having a very religious upbringing in a very happy home atmosphere, as Christianity was the basic standard of family life. The first thing every morning was family worship and prayer, and again last thing at night before retiring to bed. No one dare lie or go to bed before family worship took place, unless they were ill. Sundays were strictly observed as the Lord's Day. There was a morning service at eleven a.m., Sunday school at three p.m., followed by an evening service at six p.m. No work of any kind was done on Sunday, except cooking your meals. Even the water was drawn from the wells on the Saturday and stored in pails to last all the Sabbath day. One was allowed to roam the hills and glens in between services and we, the youth of the village, would climb the hills and look over the cliffs at the birds which nested there and on the rocks, far down below, in their thousands, but we were not allowed any kind of play.

The village nestled at the foot of the hills; the highest and my favourite is called Conachair. The cliff side, which is a sheer drop of 1397 feet, was covered with nesting birds. As you watch the Atlantic's rolling waves dashing against the cliffs, it can be very exciting. One can get a panoramic view of the island, and smaller islets like Boreray, Stac Lee and Stac an Armin; on the other side Soay, Levenish and on a clear day the Outer Hebrides of Lewis, Harris and Benbecula. Clinging to the side of each hill and glen like limpets to a rock on the seashore are hundreds of cleits, where our stores of peats were kept. Around the village there are also cleits where hay was kept for cattle. There are stone dykes around the village to keep sheep out, and also stone built gardens where poorer sheep are put for better grazing.

The houses of the village were elongated along the main street, overlooking a large, natural bay. All the houses were built to conform: one large kitchen, one large bedroom and a smaller bedroom. In between the two was a small lobby as you enter.

Conachair – the highest hill on St Kilda. Clinging like limpets to a rock, hundreds of cleits are found on every hill and inside the head dyke to the back of the village (Alasdair MacEachen)

These were called 'Crofters' Houses'. There was not a lot of space for a large family, and when all our family were at home, some of us had to sleep in the byre.

My father was very religious, as was my mother. On Sundays it was his duty to ring the church bell, calling the villagers to the church service, and he was also the 'Precentor' who led the congregation's singing in Gaelic. My father was always the last to leave church, and in the winter he had to light the paraffin lamps before the service and extinguish them when the service was over. After the rest of the congregation had gone home, I sat in our pew till all the lights were put out and my father had lit the storm lantern. My father would then tell me to kneel beside him while he prayed, then he would ask me to say the Lord's Prayer in Gaelic. After, we would walk hand in hand home, which was about half a mile from the church. My reason for stopping behind to accompany him was that in my boyish mind, I thought I would be of some comfort to him in the dark, after being told so many ghost stories, which, as a child, I truly believed.

Once I had an unusual experience. I was eight years old and in bed, sandwiched in between two of my brothers. The night was very warm and I could not sleep, so I got out from under the blankets and sat on the pillow. My brothers were fast asleep and so were my father and mother who were also in the same room. All of a sudden I heard banging on the window several times; it was quite dark and it sounded as if something was being pushed through the window, and then suddenly I heard the most awful scream. I was petrified and got under the blankets as fast as I could, and yet nobody else heard a thing. Some four years later, my sister Christina died and as her coffin was passed through the same window, my mother gave such a scream. The thought passed through my mind of the similarity to what I had heard on the night four years previously. It could have been a bird, but I cannot think of any bird that would act in such a peculiar way, so I leave the subject to one's imagination. 'Is there such a thing as a ghost?'

Chapter 1

As a boy I never wore boots or shoes – only the elderly people wore any, except in winter time, so that as a result our feet were like tough leather. We were allowed one pair of tackety boots a year; sometimes they had to last two years and even the young women in their teens had to go barefoot throughout the summer months. Each family had their own sheep and each also had its special marking, made in the ears of each lamb at birth, and at a distance one could tell who the owner was. Also, naturally, each had at least one cow, and in the case of a large family, two cows to provide enough milk, butter and our own special kind of cheese. If a family should not have enough milk the neighbours provided a pint free each day. Our main staple food was, of course, 'salt mutton', fulmars, gannets and potatoes. In the spring, when the puffins, guillemots and razorbills arrived from their emigration, we slaughtered them in their hundreds for fresh food and for their feathers. They were fat and nutritious, and their eggs were also collected, which added to our food variety. They were enjoyable to eat, whether boiled, fried or made into a kind of omelette. The puffins' eggs looked and tasted very much like chickens' eggs, but they were very difficult to get, as the puffin lays its eggs in burrows under the ground. One would often get nasty nips and cuts by putting his hand in a puffin's burrow, for he guarded his eggs so well.

The eggs we did not make use of were emptied of their contents by boring a small hole in the side of the shell with a special round file, inserting a small blow pipe in the egg, and blowing by the mouth till it was empty of white and yolk. We sold these to tourists or any stranger who cared to buy them, at two pence each. They varied in size and colour according to the species and made nice ornaments.

The main industry of the island was, of course, the making of the famous St Kilda tweed. It was all done by hand, from the shearing of the sheep to the finished, produced tweed. It was a long, monotonous process and the long winter months were occupied by the making of the tweed. Long after the younger members of the family had gone to bed, the parents and the older members of the family worked until two in the morning, and started again at seven the following morning.

As I recall, life was very hard and all heavy work had to be carried out by manual means. There was no modern equipment, no electricity and no gas. In order to plant corn and potatoes, we had to dig the ground with a spade and plant everything by hand. We would dig peat, which is the traditional fuel of the Highlands, by going out into the moors and cutting out large lumps of top earth; this was then dried by exposure to the air and once dried it was ready for burning. Grass and corn cutting was carried out by hand; everything that had to be carried was transported on one's back. There were no donkeys or horses on the island. Some of the women were as strong as the men, and they had to carry just as heavy a load, so in this sense they truly had their 'equal rights'. The difference between the men and the women was that the women were never allowed to scale the cliffs in order to collect the birds' eggs, nor were they allowed to go out in the rowing boats. However, I can remember that on certain occasions when the wildfowlers were visiting the smaller islands, some of the young girls were allowed to accompany the men. I have seen two of my sisters and a female cousin on such a trip but this was a very rare occasion.

When we went fishing we would row out to many small caves that were dotted round the island. We would then row into one of these caves, which were as large as caverns. We would use handlines instead of fishing rods, and our usual catch consisted mainly of bream. Sometimes when we entered a cave we would surprise some seals which were lazing on ledges just above the waterline. On our approach, they would dive into the water and disappear beneath the waves. Perched on the higher ledges were thousands of seabirds: guillemots, razorbills, cormorants, fulmars, kittiwakes, gulls and wild ducks. These birds would fly in and out non-stop and the sound of thousands of flapping wings and the screeching of the different species was wonderful to listen to, especially at nesting time.

Chapter 1

Looking from our boat we could see their eggs and later, on visits to the same caves, we would see the hatched young. The parent birds would fly in and out with their beaks full of food for their young. I always wondered why they never collided as the air was literally full of flapping wings.

The islanders would collect large quantities of the wild birds' eggs for their own consumption when they were accessible, but there were also thousands that were inaccessible.

It was every boy's ambition to visit the islands around St Kilda collecting the eggs in early spring. All the men and boys took part in this operation and we visited all the stacs, even though some were very difficult and dangerous to land on. Although it was considered hazardous, it was our way of life from generation to generation. On one such occasion I lost an uncle over one of the cliffs, and also a friend who was with him.

On this occasion, the cliffs, which were known by name, had been divided up among the community; this meant systematic coverage of the nesting places. The men would be lowered down the cliff by rope and they would then catch the young fulmars which were killed and salted and as such provided the islanders with a year round diet. The young fulmar is very nutritious, being very fat and oily, and was an excellent food for the long, cold winter. The cliffs had been allocated by pulling from a cap a piece of paper with the name of a part of the cliff on it. The head of the family would make the draw. Where it was a one-man family or where a man's family were not yet old enough to go down the cliffs he would team up with another family and together they would share their parts of the cliff.

It was in this manner that my uncle had joined with his friend to work as partners. No one will ever know what happened. My uncle's friend's body was recovered wedged between the rocks far below the cliffs, and my uncle's body was never found. We believed the rope must have snapped between them and my uncle fell to the sea below. The whole island was shocked and grieved for many a day.

In my father's day life was much harder than when I was a boy. I have mentioned earlier how we went wildfowling in order to catch birds, which were our main, staple food. Well, in earlier times these birds were even more essential to the diet of the St Kildans.

The men visited all the sea stacs around the main island as these precipitous pillars often provided excellent pickings of gannets and guillemots. At dark they would approach the stacs and from rowing boats, spring onto the steep rocks. Then, gripping the rock with their fingers and digging their toes into the narrow cracks, they ascended to the top of the cliff or the ledge the birds were nesting on. At their approach most of the birds would take to the air. The men would then take up their position and wait for the birds to return. When dusk had passed and darkness approached, the birds would return for the night. At first the birds would approach the nesting place and circle three times, before assuring themselves that all was clear and finally settling down. First one would land, then the others would follow in groups, until the ledge was crammed with birds.

One bird would take over as guard while the other birds slept with their heads tucked under a wing. The first job was to catch the sentry off guard. If he let out his piercing cry to warn the other birds, then the whole night's work would have been wasted. One of the men would creep up behind the lookout while holding his breath, so as not to alert the bird. When near enough, the wildfowler would make his move and grab the bird's beak with one hand and his neck with the other. A sudden twist backwards and the neck was broken. It was easy then to catch the sleeping birds and kill them. They were then collected by the boatman and the wildfowlers would make their descent.

Another ambition of every boy was to be lowered down the cliff like his father and older brothers to catch a fulmar. A rope was tied around your waist and your father or your big brother lowered you down the cliff face, while your mother and sisters cheered you on. It was very frightening when you were the person being lowered over the cliff, for far below you could hear the raging sea crashing against the rocks. Occasionally your foothold would slip and then you would be swinging at the end of the rope with anything between a 300 feet and 1000 feet drop beneath you, but this initial fright soon disappeared after you had made two or three descents.

On one occasion I nearly lost my young life. I was about five years old when I asked my eldest brother to lower me down a cliff to catch a fulmar in its nest. It was during the time of the year we call the fulmar harvest, and the whole family was present. My father and brother were after killing all the birds they could carry home for that day and were getting ready to leave. My brother was none too keen to oblige my request but I persisted by asking my father to tell John to lower me down. Finally he relented and said, 'Come on, I will lower you down but, you'd better catch a fulmar.' The rope was tied in a lasso around my waist and I was lowered down. It was difficult to get a foothold with my bare feet. The cliff was almost perpendicular; I dug my toes into small grooves in the face of the rock and clung on with my small fingers. As I descended opposite to the nest, the young fulmar watching my descent became restless, and it hissed and spumed all over my face. I drew back, for I did not like the oily spume which had been squirted all over me. I tried several times but the bird defended itself admirably. Everyone above kept shouting, 'Go on, catch it.' My brother, meanwhile, was becoming impatient at my antics; he gave a sharp tug of the rope and before I could retrieve my position, I was hanging upside down. From my upright position I was now looking down onto the bottom rocks and the foaming sea. Everyone was shouting and bawling at my brother to stop pulling me up as I now began slipping through the noose. The rope slipped around my knees; I held on with my hands for dear life, but it was becoming a terrific strain. I was being banged against the cliff and getting caught on the jagged rocks which protruded from the rock face. The noose had tightened round my ankles and I doubled up, before I finally felt my brother's strong hands pull me clear of danger. My poor mother and sisters, who had been watching all the time, were weeping. Everyone was sure I would die. I later learned that my brother had been terribly frightened that he would never pull me up in time, but I remember he kept encouraging me all the time to hold on: even though he knew that with every inch he pulled me up I was slipping further through the rope. When he had pulled me to safety, he said: 'That is the last time I will ever lower you down.' He then walked off on his own; I can only imagine what his thoughts must have been at that moment.

As for myself, I cannot remember being scared during this particular incident; I was only frightened that I would be scolded for not catching the bird. However, I soon forgot about the incident and went down several times after that. There were two other occasions on which I nearly lost my life, but I shall relate later on the times when I believe 'Providence' saved me.

Chapter 2

My father's name was William; my mother was Mary Ann (MacQueen). They had married in 1895 when my father was twenty and my mother was four years older. Eleven children came from the marriage, of which eight are still alive. These are Finlay, Annabella, Mary, Finlay John, Calum (self), Rachel, Marion and Mae. The three of the family who died were John, Mary-Betsy and Kirsty. It was quite a large family to have raised under such circumstances, as it would be even today. My father had little money coming in, but with the proceeds from the tweed that we made, we were able to live quite well. Our diet consisted of birds' eggs, salted seabirds and sometimes

WIDOWS ORPHANS AND OLD AGE CONTRIBUTORY PENSIONS ACT, 1925.

CERTIFICATE OF MARRIAGE.

When and Where Married.	Names of Parties.	Rank or Profession.	Age.
1895. Eighteenth June	William Macdonald (Cragsman) Bachelor	Cragsman	20 years
St. Kilda	Mary Ann McQueen (Domestic Servant) Spinster	Domestic Servant	24 years

I hereby certify that the above particulars are extracted by me from Entry No. 2 in the Register Book of Marriages pertaining to the District of St. Kilda in the County of Inverness for the year 1895.

(Place) St Kilda Donald Cameron Registrar.

(Date) 14th November 1925.

(2527) Wt 5035/39 10,000 8/25 M. & Sn. Ltd. G 25.

William MacDonald's marriage certificate (John MacDonald)

fish we had caught. It was good, staple food and we never went hungry.

Naturally, at times we went short of some items which we could not grow ourselves, such as sugar, tea, oatmeal and flour. We never went hungry though, and father always bought flour and oatmeal in bulk. My mother and sisters did all the baking: flour-scones and oatcakes; as long as we had these in our home we were always full.

Our supplies in the summer came from Glasgow, but in the winter we depended upon the fishing trawlers which often sheltered in St Kilda bay, or called on their way to and from the fishing grounds. These boats came from Fleetwood, Hull and Aberdeen; many of them were great friends. In the winter they would bring us anything that we were short of. They also acted as our mailmen and would take or bring us any letters that needed delivering. To us young boys there was always great excitement when the trawlers came into the bay for a short stay; on occasions there were as many as twenty boats at anchor. We used to go from one boat to another and received many a titbit from the cooks: large mugs of tea, sometimes a slice of cake which was really a treat. Cake was unheard of on the island and so were most sweet things. The fishermen were real friends and would give us anything that they could spare. Sometimes we would return their kindness by taking them fresh eggs or a pair of knitted socks.

I can remember the first day at school; I was thrilled at the very idea of going to school and I continued to like learning very much. Naturally, I found it difficult at first, especially as lessons were taught in English and I was only used to talking in Gaelic. The early days were spent learning the letters of the alphabet, then I progressed onto two-letter words, then more difficult words followed. The teacher, who was the wife of the missionary, wrote on a blackboard with chalk and I was given a slate and pencil with which to copy her writings.

After this came sums: adding, subtracting, multiplying and dividing. I found it very complicated as I was thinking in Gaelic

The schoolroom (right) and church (left) with the Kirk bell
(Alasdair MacEachen)

and trying, as I could only speak in Gaelic, to communicate with my teacher in English but she was very patient. Occasionally her husband, the missionary, took over the school when his wife was away. There were two boys in my class, the sons of the village nurse. She was an Edinburgh woman and her sons were very bright and they could speak nothing but English, therefore they had an advantage over the rest of us other children. In later years one became a doctor and the other, a lawyer. Mr Cameron, our teacher, realised the advantage that the two boys had over the rest of us. He took me aside: 'Listen to me, Calum, I know you try very hard to learn and keep up with Ian and if you had the same chance as him in life, you would be just as good as him. You think in Gaelic and try to put the context into English, therefore he has the answer to the question before you. Do not be disheartened at his quickness to answer the question before you, as you are as bright as him. Just keep studying and you will get on.' We then returned to class. I think that little talk helped me a great deal throughout my life.

Each morning school began with prayers and then we had a certain subject to write about. No one was allowed to speak to the other pupils during school hours. The rules were very strict and if you were caught talking or generally being mischievous you would be caned or strapped across the hands with a leather belt.

I remember on one occasion a girl cousin and myself were larking about when the teacher looked up and caught us. We were ordered to the middle of the floor and told to put out our hands for the cane. My cousin did as she was bid; I, however, refused. It didn't matter how much the teacher coerced me, I would not give in and put out my hand. I was made to stand in the corner for two hours and finally I was kept behind after school. In the end I had to receive a light caning on the hand. A week or so later the teacher and her husband came up to the village to call on all the parents to give them year-end reports on their children. Naturally my parents asked how I was progressing. 'Oh, very well,' said the woman, 'he is quite bright, but awfully stubborn.' My father enquired, 'In what way?' 'Well,' she said, 'seeing you have asked, I will tell you.' She related my obstinacy of a few weeks before and I will always remember the look on my father's face as the sorry tale unfolded. I knew that I was in for it when the couple had left. Sure enough, my father took hold of me, put me across his knee and I received six of the best across my bare behind. 'Now,' he said, 'you will do what your teacher tells you, or else.' I admit I learned my lesson and was obedient from then on. I cannot ever remember being caned during the rest of my school days.

Many a day I felt hungry and during the dinner break, from one o'clock till two, I would walk home to my house at the end of the village. Dinner did not vary very much: leg of salted fulmar and boiled potatoes or boiled mutton, and occasionally we had soup. Tea was our favourite beverage but too often this was unavailable. I remember on one occasion when our supply of tea had run out and I thought dinner would be a kind of porridge which my mother made from the fat of a fulmar and oatmeal. I hated the stuff, so instead of going home I went down to the seashore where I collected some seaweed which I began to eat. The seaweed tasted sweet and I had quite a feast. That evening when I returned home after school, my mother asked where I had been for dinner. I told her the reason for my absence and what I had eaten, and the whole family burst out laughing. 'You missed a lovely dinner,' they said. 'Your uncle came over and brought some tea, so we had mutton and potatoes and tea to finish, and now you will have to take your porridge after all. That will teach you to come home whether you like it or not.' I felt pretty mad with myself but my dear mother took me aside and said, 'Never mind, I kept your dinner and now they will have to eat their porridge.' My face beamed, for I had the last laugh after all.

My first contact with strangers took place after the 1914 war had broken out. A warship arrived in our bay and we were told that the Government was putting a naval base on the island for the duration of the war. The sailors came ashore with their

The Navy huts (Alasdair MacEachen)

equipment and set up huts close to the beach, on the land belonging to the missionary. This land and some grazing pastures were requisitioned and no one dared to object to this. Some of the islanders were engaged as a labour force. They were not paid very much but it helped the economy of the island. We also knew that the ship would call more regularly and this would bring more contact with the outside world, hopefully ensuring trade. At first the sailors kept very much to themselves and rarely communicated with the natives. However, among these strangers we found that there were two sailors who could speak Gaelic, having originated from the island of Lewis. This was wonderful news to the old men and women, for they came to our church and took part in the Gaelic service. They were invited into our homes and allowed to visit us any time they wished. In the end, we were the best of friends and strangers no longer. From then on, the ships called more frequently, usually to bring mail and supplies to the sailors.

I cannot imagine what life must have been like before my days on the island with hardly any contact with the outside world. People on the island were now able to travel to the mainland and the isles of Lewis and Harris with trips provided by the visiting ships. My father often travelled to Lewis and Harris and sometimes as far as Aberdeen and Glasgow. It was an entirely different world to them and as children we would listen in awe at the tales they told on their return. I remember my father telling of one of his experiences when he returned from a trip to Lewis and Harris, a journey of fifty-six miles. He started on his journey and had only gone a short way when he was overtaken by a gypsy caravan. They stopped and asked my father where he was heading, so he told them Stornoway, Isle of Lewis. They offered to give him a lift and my father was a bit apprehensive at first as he was not sure of their intentions. Inside were all the family and their worldly goods, but he feared he might be robbed although he only had a few pounds on him. However, he inwardly prayed and took courage that he would be safe on the journey. He was soon surprised by the courtesy shown him by these thoroughly hospitable people, for they even took time to prepare him a meal. Finally they reached their destination, and when my father offered to pay for the lift and meal, they would hear none of it, saying it was their pleasure. They wished him a good holiday and bade him farewell. From that moment on my father would not hear a word said against any gypsies and he would always say, 'They are human beings just like the rest of us.'

Chapter 3

We made our own fun and sports by roaming the hills and shore. We had lovely, sandy beaches when the tide was out but we were never allowed to go too far out in the sea, as there was always the danger from sharks, and as a result none of us learned to swim. I can remember seeing sharks stranded on the beach when the tide had gone out quickly, with the result that the sharks were left high and dry.

As a boy on St Kilda, I think my greatest thrill occurred in summer 1916, when I was eight years old. My father asked me if I would like to go fishing with him and the other men of the island. One condition that I would have to accept if I went was that I would still go to school as usual the following morning at nine-thirty. This I readily agreed to do.

Fishing on these occasions would last all night and we would return to the village the next morning. Every family on the island possessed a deep fishing line which was anything up to 200 yards in length. At intervals of about one yard there extended a string, attached to which was a four inch hook. Four families shared each of the four rowing boats that the community as a whole owned.

Every man of the crew took water and tea in two ordinary glass bottles. There were also buttered scones, oatcakes, salt mutton and homemade cheese to eat for supper and breakfast. The crew on this particular occasion consisted of seven strong men, each with a canvas bag filled with hay. This was to be their sleeping bag for the night. Each man also had a blanket. In the rowing boat there was also a sail in case there was a wind to assist the rowers. Last but not least in the boat's inventory, there was a bible.

So we set out one evening, six men rowing and one man steering. The rowers alternated with the steerer in order to have a spell of rest. The boat moved further and further into the waters of the Atlantic, and the island shrank smaller and smaller with each pull on the oars. At last, when we were about four miles out to sea, we stopped and began setting our fishing lines down. To each end of the fishing lines was attached a buoy with a red flag protruding from the top of it. When all the lines had been laid out, we rowed back to Dun. Dun is an island which makes up the bay and is separated from the main island by a narrow sound, which can only be crossed by boat. It has several small caves eaten into it by the constant battering of the Atlantic rollers. There is one cave, however, which is cavernous inside. It has two entrances and is dog-legged in shape. The sea inside this cave was very calm if the wind was from the east or north-east. This was to be our home and shelter for the night. We arrived about ten p.m., and anchored in the centre of the cave.

I looked around in awe at its walls of sheer rock. On the ledges just above the waterline there had been resting some seals, but on our arrival they tumbled into the water and disappeared from sight. In the numerous cracks and crevices there were thousands of seabirds. The noise they made was deafening as they flew in and out all night. Though it was still quite bright outside, the inside of the cave was fairly dark. After anchoring, the men took out their food parcels. Before supper, however, grace was said. Conversation then revolved around what we might catch the following morning.

I did not take part in this conversation; I was more interested in the life going on all around me and the thrill of it all. After supper was ended and packed away, the bible was taken out. We all started to sing a psalm and it reminded me of the church as the sound echoed throughout the cave. Most of the birds took fright and abandoned their nests, not to return until the service was over. After a chapter from the New Testament was read, we all knelt on the bottom of the boat and my father said the evening prayers. Afterwards we rose up and climbed into our sleeping bags. We were packed like sardines, head to feet. Our day clothes were kept on and a blanket covered each of us. My father made me comfortable and asked me if I would like to be at home in my own bed. 'Oh no,' I said, 'this night I shall never forget.' During the night I could not sleep one wink. I could hear snoring from the others in the boat and the din from the birds was indescribable. The sea was lapping against our boat as we circled around our anchor and with my general excitement sleep was an impossibility.

At that time of the summer, the nights in the far north are very short, lasting only two or three hours. At four a.m. everyone was awake but feeling rather stiff and sore as a result of the crammed conditions on board. Everyone was concerned as to how I had slept. 'Not a wink,' I said. They all laughed and said they thought that the music of the birds would have put me to sleep. The sleeping bags were soon packed away. The bible was taken out once again and a service started the same as the night before. After this the box containing the leftover food was brought out and we had breakfast, which was washed down by cold tea. When this was completed we weighed anchor and rowed out of the cave. My father told me to row with him to warm myself up and to get my blood circulating, which I did. After an hour's hard rowing we reached the place where the markers were bobbing about on the ocean. I looked over the side of the boat in order to catch the first glimpse of the catch as it came into view from the darkness below. Suddenly I saw a voluminous shape approaching the bottom of the boat. It was spiralling around and around and when it broke the surface, I saw it was a halibut, the largest I had ever seen. It was over five feet in length and nearly as broad. The men had great difficulty getting the fish aboard and it was not until it was finally gaffed near the tail and a rope was tied around its body that we finally succeeded. We now had such a heavy catch that the gunwale of the boat was nearly level with the sea. We packed away the fishing lines and rowed back to St Kilda bay. On reaching our island all the fish was salted and preserved for a later occasion. All, that is, except the halibut, for that was too large to salt. Instead, it was cut up and divided among the families on the island.

When the boat had touched shore I left the fishermen and made my way home for I would have to be at school by nine-thirty. My mother was waiting for me and she embraced me, asking, 'How did the trip go? Did you manage to sleep?' 'No,' was my reply, 'but I must get ready for school.' 'Not today,' she said firmly, 'it is straight to bed for you.'

I slept until late in the afternoon, and when I finally got up my father was getting ready for another night's fishing. 'I see you did not go to school this morning after all,' he said. 'Mother wouldn't let me' was my reply, rather sheepishly. 'Ah well, that is the last time you will go out night fishing until you are grown up.' Although for a different reason I never did go out again night fishing, I shall never forget the thrill and the experience of that one night spent on the sea.

Chapter 4

In 1913 my eldest brother John left home for Glasgow to take up employment in the city. My family and the islanders gathered to say goodbye and we were all sad. My father did not object as there was no work on the island and it was plain to see that his future lay elsewhere. My youngest sister had not been born at the time and it was an especially sad occasion as this was the first break in the family, although one sister had died before I was born.

When World War I broke out in 1914, we had a letter from my brother in Glasgow saying that he was joining the Army. The news upset my parents very much. They had fears for his life as any parent would. The word soon passed around the village, and all our neighbours came to our house sympathising and offering encouragement. 'Have faith, God will look after him,' they said; but mother was overcome with grief and sadness thinking she would not see her son again. I was about six years old then and could not grasp what all the fuss was about; neither could I grasp the fact that in the outside world a nation was fighting another nation. To me, St Kilda was my world. No other land was in view, only a great expanse of water, the Atlantic, as far as the eye could see. Only when I climbed to the heights of the mountain could I see the hazy outline of Harris, and even then it had to be a very clear day. Ships often passed in the distance and trawlers came into the bay.

From my school maps I knew that there was land and there were people living in countries out there beyond the horizon. Compared to the isles of Lewis and Harris, our nearest neighbours, St Kilda was a mere pin dot on the map. Naturally, as I got older I was inquisitive about the outside world, but could not comprehend the vastness of the other countries as compared to my world.

I can still remember the first Army leave my brother John ever received. He had been stationed in France during the war and was

John MacDonald, St Kilda – the only St Kildan to serve in Gallipoli in World War I. Due to the difficulty in getting to St Kilda he only got to spend four hours there out of his two weeks leave on his return from Gallipoli (John MacDonald)

given a week's leave. It took him nearly three days to journey to St Kilda, with the result that he had only eight hours to spend with his family before he had to leave the island in order to return to his unit before his furlough ran out. We had not been expecting him as we had not received a letter from him for a long time. My father was away visiting one of the small islands with the rest of the able-bodied men and he was not expected home till late that evening.

We first noticed the trawler as it came into the bay and it had anchored before we realised that there was a soldier on board. My mother and sisters were all very excited and the remaining villagers began to gather around the house. The Navy sailors stationed near the shore set out in their boats to meet the captain and crew. When we saw the soldier descending into the rowing boat everyone made a rush for the quay. I was left at home to mind my baby sister and was very disappointed not to be present when the soldier stepped ashore. I had only been five years old when I had last seen my brother and now I was eight. As I watched the procession coming towards me I was overcome with excitement. My mother and my sisters were clinging to his arms with the rest of the family following. When he was near enough he bent down and picked me up. I felt rather shy as he was more like a stranger to me than a brother. Compared with the rest of the men he looked rather smart in his uniform and I was really proud of him.

When we realised that father was not present and he would not know of the homecoming of his son there was a bit of a commotion. No one knew how to get word to him. An old man left the party and began to walk up the hill. He walked the whole length of the island to where the island of Soay juts out from the furthest part of St Kilda. Soay itself is separated from the main island by a narrow sound which can only be crossed by a small boat. The man scaled down the cliff to where some men were manning a rowing boat as a ferry. He shouted to the men what was happening; they in turn passed the message on to my father.

My father left the men on the island in the boat, and was put ashore to hear the news first hand from the old man. Finally the old man told my father: 'You go on, I shall follow.' It was a long walk over the moorland and hills. When he was in view of the village side of the hills, my mother told John to go and meet his father.

Everyone was watching their encounter; the distance between them narrowed until finally they embraced. We watched as they knelt down and prayed in thanksgiving. After a while they rose and walked down through the village. It was a really happy event in my early life. John had one more leave the following year; however, on this occasion he was able to spend four days with his family. He was always remembered in all our prayers both in the church and in every home on the island. He joined the Army at the outbreak of the war and was demobilised in 1919, at the age of twenty-three, and I am glad to say that in that time was never wounded. Our prayers were truly answered.

We did not have any sort of music on the island and no one ever learned to dance until the Navy station was installed in 1914. The Navy men would give a party for the young women and children at Christmas time. It was a great occasion. The huts where the party was to be held were gaily decorated with flags about the walls and bunting. New games were taught to the children and we were given chocolate, sweets and Christmas stockings. Everyone had a wonderful time singing and dancing.

There was a particular Navy man called Crockston who took a particular liking to me. He was very fatherly, with a pointed beard. Often, when he was visiting our house, he would take me on his knee and tell me stories about his trips, hiking and camping before the war, when he had been a Scout Master. Whenever he went on leave he would ask me what I would like to be brought back as a present, a toy boat or model train. I was the envy of all the boys when I showed them my presents from Crockston.

At the time the Navy were first stationed on St Kilda there were no girls of flirtation age on the island. My eldest sister, Annie, was herself only fourteen and Mary, the next in line, was two years younger. By 1919, when the Navy men were to be withdrawn, there were quite a few girls who had reached maturity and many a young love affair had developed. Often I came across young couples kissing and cuddling. I was told, under threat of a clip around my ear, to keep my mouth closed.

An amusing incident occurred one day involving my sister Annie. I had been spinning bobbins which are required for tweed making, when into the room walked Annie. In one hand she had a red book, in the other a saucer of flour. She made straight for the mirror upon the mantelpiece and started putting flour on her face with a damp cloth. When she had whitened her face she proceeded to rub the damp cloth on the red cloth of the book. As the dye came off the book she smeared the 'rouge' onto her face and lips. I said, 'What in the world are you doing, Annie?' 'Never you mind, get on with your work' was the reply. 'Ah,' I said, 'you are in love with the sailor man and I am going to tell.' Annie's face blushed scarlet. 'Please don't tell on me, I have read in books that women all over the world put powder and rouge on their face and lips to make them pretty; so that is what I am doing.' 'But,' I said, 'you look awful.' She kissed my cheek, turned on her heels and marched out of the room. Of course, I never did tell on her but I have often reminded her of the incident and we have a good laugh over it.

The towering cliffs of St Kilda were very important to the Navy during the four years of the war as they provided excellent positions for keeping track of shipping and enemy submarines. The two strategic lookout posts were on hills called Oiseval and Mullach Mor. Oiseval was manned by the Navy and Mullach Mor by the St Kildans. The view from these two vantage points extended for miles out to sea. Any movements were notified by telephone to the naval station and noted in a log-book by the man on duty up the hill. Many merchant ships passed the island plying to and from America, and sometimes German submarines were spotted. In the vicinity of St Kilda numerous ships were sunk by these submarines, torpedoes or deck guns. The crews of the unfortunate ships came to our islands in their lifeboats and were taken care of by the Navy until a ship was sent from the mainland to transport them back to Scotland. The caves around the island were full of flotsam and wreckage from the doomed merchant ships. The natives went around all the accessible caves and salvaged everything of value. Barrels of oil, crates of candles, boxes of cigarettes and planks of wood would be towed ashore to supplement the St Kildans' spartan mode of life. The naval personnel did not intervene or claim any finds so we were at liberty to sell the oil to merchants on the mainland and use the candles in our homes.

St Kilda Reference Number 1 19[illegible]

Date of Receipt. (1)	Estimated Value. (2)	Description of Property. (3)
Nov 15th 1918		1 case of chloroform
Name and Address of Owners (if known). (4) D. Flockhart & Co Edinburgh		
Name, Official No., and Port of Registry of Ship (if known). (5)		

Particulars of Salvage.

Date when found. (6)	Exact spot where found. (7)
July 15th 1916	North side of the Island of Soa High and dry on the rocks above low water mark
Services rendered. (8)	Recovered by climbing down the cliff could not be salved from the sea
Names of Salvor. (9)	Address of Salvor. (10)
Neil Ferguson	No. 6 Main St St Kilda

Wr. 16. *Note.*—The Receiver is referred to his Instructions as to payment of Salvors in advance.

Extract from the Receiver of Wreck's records detailing a find by Neil Ferguson on 15th July 1916
(Alasdair MacEachen)

Our best find was a cask of rum. It was shared out among all the heads of each family and stored in every bottle or utensil one could find. When we ran out of bottles the remainder was left in the charge of the Postmaster and locked in his byre. Alcohol was only used on the island for medicinal purposes like treating colds and flu. On this special occasion some of the older men folk took more than was good for them and they became very jolly and happy, but no one got drunk. In the end most of the rum was used to entertain the tourists or strangers who visited the island long after the war ended.

We nearly found another cask of alcohol on another occasion. My father and Annie had gone up the hills to look for sheep to take home and slaughter for the family's meals. They had looked over the cliffs and seen far below on one of the beaches a large cask. My father told Annie to stay back from the edge of the cliff while he went down to investigate. He tied the rope he carried to a rock and lowered himself down to the beach below. To his disappointment he found that it was a wine cask, but empty. The underside of the cask had been cracked by the pounding of the sea and the rocks upon which the cask now rested were coloured red by the liquid which had oozed out. He looked upwards and seeing Annie near the cliff edge, beckoned to her to move back. Annie mistook his sign to mean go and get help. Off she went running like the wind over land and glen. When my father reached the top he looked around but not a sign of Annie could be seen. Realising what must have happened he began to run after her. He soon caught sight of her but she was too far away to hear him shouting for her to stop. He knew he must stop her before she spread the news and someone launched the boat which would mean a four hour round trip to no avail for somebody. He kept after her but could not close the gap. Annie was still breaking all records at running. She arrived home breathless and managed to tell the great news. They were getting ready to launch the boat when my father appeared over the ridge. He was now walking slowly. He was tired out when he reached home. 'Oh Annie, Annie, you nearly killed me running and shouting after you. The cask was empty. I only waved you back from the edge of the cliff.' Everyone burst out laughing except for poor Annie who only felt a fool. However, the incident was soon forgotten.

On another occasion a misadventure nearly resulted in myself and my brother, Finlay John, losing our lives. The incident occurred one day after we had finished school. Finlay John, who was two years older than me at the time, said, 'Shall we climb over Oiseval [one of the high hills on St Kilda]?' I agreed so off we went. On this particular day a sea mist was covering most of the higher slopes of the hills and this added to our sense of adventure. We were hoping to climb as high as the naval lookout point and

Oiseval in the background (Alasdair MacEachen)

pay the Navy men a surprise visit. We did not go home to tell our parents our intentions as we knew the route very well. As we climbed higher and higher the mist which had been rolling down the lower slopes thickened and we were unable to see very far in front of us. Still we climbed, unaware of any imminent danger. We had come to the part of the hills called the Gap. We knew that to our left there was a perpendicular drop straight into the sea which, although we could not see, we could hear crashing far below. To our right we knew that if we followed the ridge of the cliff we would find the path which would lead to the summit. The cliffs at this particular point were especially treacherous as they followed a zigzag pattern and one had to have his wits about him so as not to fall. As all boys will do, we began to dare each other to see who was the bravest. We each agreed to close our eyes and carry on climbing. The loser, of course, was the one who opened his eyes first. We held each other's hand and began to feel our way along as best we could. 'Have you opened your eyes?', one would say to the other. 'No, have you?' was the reply. We went on for a while, back and forth, the question answered by a question. We were each beginning to feel uneasy and had less bravado with each step we took. Suddenly I stopped. I could not go on for there seemed to be some invisible force telling me not to move. Even if I had wanted to I doubt that I could take another step. Intuitively I knew that I must go no further. 'Come on,' urged Finlay John, 'why have you stopped? Have you opened your eyes?' 'No, but I am going to do so now,' I said. Sure enough it was fate which had made me stop and open my eyes. One step away from our feet was nothing but thin air. We were standing in front of a yawning chasm. Our bodies would never have been found, as we would have fallen as surely as my uncle had, into the sea. From our knowledge of Oiseval we knew that the sea would have been over 600 feet below. We ran away from the edge and continued our way to the top. No one was ever told of our escapade in case it came to our parents' ears and we would have got the hiding of our lives.

Chapter 4

Another time when I believe fate played a part in saving my life occurred soon after this incident. I believe I would have been drowned but for the help of a greater power. It was in the same summer and also after school had finished for the day. I was on my way home when I met my second eldest brother Finlay who was eleven years older than me. With my brother was a first cousin who lived next door to us. They were both engaged as native lookouts by the Navy. They usually took watch at a place called Ruaival. Looking from the bay it seemed to be part of Dun which makes up the whole bay. However, it is divided from Dun by a sea channel. At low tide this channel is so narrow that you have to push through it in a boat by using the sides of the rocks. It can be an extremely dangerous place to be caught in if the sea is rough and the Atlantic rollers start to thunder into this narrow gap.

My uncle, who worked a different shift as a watchman, had spotted a barrel bobbing almost submerged in a sea cave. To

Looking out to Dun channel from the doorway of the family home, No. 3 Main Street (Alasdair MacEachen)

get to this cave would be very difficult as we would have to pass through the channel near Dun. I did not know that it was their intention to salvage this barrel so when they asked me if I would like to go for a sail I naturally agreed. We launched one of the boats from the beach. It was about ten feet long with a square stern. It rode very low in the water. The two elder brothers rowed while I took the rudder. They told me to steer for the sound of Dun. As we neared the sound and the turbulent water they told me the real reason for the trip.

As no one in the village had made an attempt to get the drum, they had decided to salvage it themselves. I had not realised what I had let myself in for. As we reached the entrance I could see the white foaming cauldron.

The Atlantic rollers looked like mountains as they forced a passage between the granite walls. Great roars erupted as the waves pounded down. At first we watched the spectacle. The waves came in threes, then all was quiet until the next batch of three thundered down. As we waited for a calmer sea we discussed the danger and wondered if we would really get through the gorge without being swamped.

My uncle climbed down the rocks from his lookout point high above. He was about four yards from our boat so we enquired in which cave the drum was located. He told us but added: 'I do not think you will be able to make it. The boat is too small and if you did reach it, how are you to handle it? It is not worth the risk.' By this time I was having second thoughts. I was continually facing the waves while the other two had their backs to them. They decided that if I would steer they would try to get through. By this time I was not having any of it and told them so.

I had become slightly hysterical and told them to put me ashore at once. 'If you want to get yourselves killed, I do not,' I told them. My uncle ashore agreed with me, so finally I got my way and we all returned home. I took a lot of abuse from both of them. My father on our return asked where we had been. When he heard the story he was furious. 'You must have been mad. You could have been drowned just for the sake of a drum of oil.' But their pride had been hurt and I got blamed for the one that got away.

One recollection that will always stay in my mind occurred one morning as I was preparing for school. It was about eight a.m. when word came from the naval station that a submarine had been sighted heading towards the bay by the watchman on Oiseval. As no British submarines were known to be in the area we were advised to take to the hills. We did as we were bid and I followed an aunt until we reached halfway up the hill behind the village. We stopped to watch the submarine as it slowly entered the mouth of the harbour. She stopped her engines at this point and did not enter any further. We had never seen a submarine before and wondered at its strange shape compared to the trawlers and other vessels with which we were familiar. All of a sudden we heard the boom of her guns followed by the splash as a shell exploded close to the shore. 'Oh! The devils,' my aunt exclaimed, 'they are trying to kill us.' 'Run, run, run for your lives. Put the hills between us,' someone shouted. We had never heard such a terrible noise as those guns made and we were terrified. We kept running up the hills until we thought we were safe. Other families arrived and most were frightened out of their wits. Still the submarine kept up the barrage; the cattle were going mad. They were running all over the hills in a stampede. The old folk were praying and the young women huddled together. Then after what seemed an eternity the firing stopped and a great silence followed. The submarine began to slither away but the men thought she might return so we were told to stay where we were. The submarine had now moved out of St Kilda bay, keeping close to the shore around the island. An old man standing high on the cliff edge waved his walking stick in a futile gesture. 'I wish this was a gun,' he shouted, 'I would shoot you right now, you devils.' We watched her moving out to sea far below. Our gaze returned to some of the crew on the conning tower, who could see us on the majestic cliffs far above them. When the submarine was far out to sea, the most spritely of the men and women took courage to return to the village. The old people and the young were not allowed to leave the sanctuary of the hills at that time.

In all, the Germans had fired seventy-two rounds of ammunition into the village. The only casualty, though, was a two-day-old lamb which had been killed. My father went to the village with Annie and Finlay to see the damage and to get provisions to take up the hills just in case the enemy returned. They found the naval personnel back in their stations, taking stock of the damage. When the submarine had started firing they had had no heavy armour with which to return fire as they had only been issued with rifles. The submarine was beyond the reach of rifle fire all the time she had been shooting at us and our defenceless village. The wireless station had been damaged. One shell went right through the church, another landed ten yards in front of our house and another blew a crater behind our houses. My uncle's house, which was next to ours, was half demolished and next to his, the whole house lay in ruins.

After my father had surveyed the damage he returned to our house and prepared a meal to take up to the hills, as we were

House No. 1 damaged by the German submarine
(Alasdair MacEachen)

not allowed to return till the following day. During the night the wireless station was repaired, a message was sent out to naval headquarters at Stornoway on the Isle of Lewis and armoured trawlers were dispatched at once to our aid. After they arrived, we returned to our normal way of life.

Chapter 5

Gradually from that day on our way of life was changed. Ships called upon us more frequently and strangers walked our street in increasing numbers. We invited these strangers into our houses and through their conversations we learned about the outside world. Some of the islanders were given free passage to the other islands and mainland of Scotland. My father would make annual visits to Stornoway and visit the families of the two Lewis naval men who were stationed on Hirta.

My father would take some tweed with him and barter for the goods we required. The families he visited also gave him gifts of dresses for my sisters and shirts with stiff 'school-collars' for us lads. Dishes of all kinds; teasets and dinner sets for mother. In fact, our home began to look very modern indeed. The delight and happiness being dressed in modern clothes gave to my sisters' lives must have been a great pleasure to my parents.

Previous to wearing such beautiful clothing the young and old women dressed in their own particular style. The dresses were made of a dark, woollen material, cut to a specified pattern by one of the natives. The style never varied from year to year. The bodice was tight fitting with a round collar and long sleeves. This buttoned down the front from the collar to the waist. A young maiden's dress, though, was buttoned down the back, and a married woman's headgear consisted of a shawl with a frilled lace and linen bonnet, while over a married woman's shoulder was worn a plaid of dark blue tweed with a red and blue thread window pane and edging. This was fastened under the throat with a round brass buckle and tied round their necks. This was normal attire and at the same time their Sunday best.

Eventually ornamental beads and jewellery were worn. These were brought to us by sailors when they returned from home leave. The whole trend began to change over later years, when even the men began wearing the modern clothes which replaced our own tailoring consisting of tweeds and second hand clothing from the mainland.

As a child I was dressed like all the other young children in a frock of material left over when my mother's dress had been made. When I was older my father made me long trousers of tweed. These were replaced after a trip my father made to the mainland by proper schoolboy trousers he had bought for me and my brothers. These were of a much finer material than the tweed and we were the envy of all the other boys in the village. All the sewing that was done, even the women's dresses, was undertaken by the men. The women folk knitted all the socks and gloves.

My father had a unique hobby on the island. This was catching wild birds and stuffing them in the tradition of a taxidermist. He sold the finished products to the Manchester Museum in return for cash, which helped to pay for the little extras that most families enjoy. I used to watch him at this job; it took about one hour to complete one bird. He made an incision under a wing then carefully worked out the insides of the bird. The body was then cut at the leg and wing joints and eventually the head. The eyes and brains were then scooped out. The skin of the bird was then cleaned up with a poisonous liquid which was kept in a bottle. Alum was then rubbed into the skin to prevent decay. After this my father stuffed wool into the bird until eventually it had resumed its original shape. The incisions were then sewn up. The wings were tied to the bird's side and it was now ready for despatch by mail to the Manchester Museum.

I was always told not to touch the poisonous liquid bottle which was kept in a cupboard in my father's bedroom. Also in this cupboard was a bottle of vinegar. The vinegar was supposed to be a remedy for sore heads, if your head ached or you had a cold. The two main medicines in every home were vinegar for sore heads and Epsom salts for any other ailment. Many a time I was given both if I was ill, just to be on the safe side. If you can imagine any place where you cannot get lemonade or mineral water you can easily acquire a taste for our thirst quenching drink. This was a glass of water with one or two drops of vinegar in it to give the drink a tang.

One night when I was spinning bobbins in the bedroom I developed a craving thirst and so I reached into the cupboard and grabbed what I thought was the vinegar bottle. I took out the cork and took a quick swig and put it back in its place. I began to feel as if my throat was burning and suddenly I realised I had drunk from the bottle of poison. I made for a pail of water in the lobby and drunk as much water as I could hold. Then I slipped outside quietly as I was feeling giddy and my insides were burning. I went back and drank more water, then went outside again. I was scared and was beginning to get panicky that someone would find out and tell my father who, after all the warnings he had given me, I felt would be furious. I went back and drank more water until I felt like bursting and returned outside again. Then I vomited and felt much better, but by now I had broken out in a sweat. After a while I felt the tension ease off. My throat was very sore although the burning sensation had lost some of its power. I returned back into the house and drank some more water. I asked my mother if I could go to bed as I was not feeling too well. 'Of course,' she said, 'you must have caught a chill; you will be alright in the morning.' Sure enough, next morning I felt fine, except for an irritation in my throat which cleared in a few days. I never told anyone of my narrow escape from being poisoned and I never touched any bottles in the cupboard after that episode. Now, every time I smell vinegar I am reminded of the childish craving I had for it that night.

All children are a bit mischievous at times and we on our lonesome isle were no exception. We had a lot of freedom, growing up. We had to make our own fun and amusement and like most children, we had a sweet tooth. As we had no shops on the island we had to make our own sweets. Sugar was not plentiful but most families had a hundred weight bag of sugar to last out the whole year. On winter nights when we went out to play, we often pinched a cupful of sugar if we had the chance. A group of us about the same age would go away up the field where there was an underground cave. It was called the Temple. We took a candle to light the inside and some dry sticks, old paper and a couple of peats and would light a fire. Someone would produce an empty syrup tin. We put the sugar we had all pinched from home into the tin. The tin was placed on the fire until the sugar became a brown, running liquid; we then added a knob of butter. When it boiled and all the sugar grains were melted, we took it off the fire and outside to a small stream. We put a flat stone in the bottom of the stream and then poured the liquefied sugar onto this slab of stone to cool, and – Hey Presto – there was our

The souterrain (earth house) or 'Fairy House' behind the village. Was this the Temple or underground cave? (Alasdair MacEachen)

sweet shop. The toffee was then divided into equal shares and put into a newspaper or a piece of cloth. We doused the fire and made for home. Seldom were we questioned as to where we got the sugar from as they had as much of a sweet tooth as we had and they just munched away at it.

One thing that was not tolerated on the island was to tell lies. One had to tell the truth whatever the cost. To steal was also unforgiveable, especially if it was from someone else outside the family. I felt the wrath of my father for these crimes on one occasion.

It was summertime and during the school holidays our teacher, her husband the missionary and their family had gone away on their annual holidays. My cousin and I were playing about on the beach making wooden boats out of pieces of driftwood we found on the shore, using our pocket knives. We shaped our boats with the knives, fixed a mast and a piece of paper for a sail and launched them into the sea. After watching them sail away we looked for small green crabs among the rocks, jumping from rock to rock just for the pleasure it gave us. When we had tired of this we walked up from the shore and looked over the missionary's garden wall. He had carrots, turnips, cabbages and potatoes growing. We took the attitude of 'When the cat's away, the mice will play.' My cousin said, 'Come on, let's pull a few carrots, they are good for eating.' I agreed with him and we did really feel a bit famished, having used all our energy playing the whole morning. So he said, 'You jump over the wall and I'll keep watch.' This I soon accomplished. I landed among the vegetables, pulled out a couple of small carrots and a turnip, then hopped back over the wall. We hid under a tarpaulin that was nearby and proceeded to scrape the carrots clean and peel the turnip, then we tucked into lunch. We munched away until we finished the lot and they were delicious. We then emerged from under the tarpaulin. No one was in sight, or so we thought. At about four o'clock we sauntered up the field towards home. As we drew near home my second eldest brother was leaning against the outside window. He was grinning and smiling at us. 'By gosh, you two are in for it, you are going to get paid for what you did,' he said. We came to a sudden halt and I asked, 'Whatever for?' 'You will soon know,' he answered. My cousin walked towards his home. My father, hearing my voice outside the house, came out in a raging mood, got hold of me by the scruff of the neck and dragged me into the house. He questioned me as to what I had been doing all morning and then asked the fateful question: 'Did you steal from the missionary's garden this morning?' I said, 'Yes, but it was only a carrot. We were hungry.' 'Well, I will teach you not to steal ever again, whether you are hungry or not.' With that he proceeded with my punishment. Today I realise I deserved all I got. Afterwards I found out that while we thought no one had seen us, an elder of the church was coming down the hillside and saw our every move. He reported it to our parents after he reached the village and we hardly ever forgave him for that.

Chapter 6

One winter event I always looked forward to was known as the night of the 'Big Carding'. This was a special occasion and each family saved some tea, sugar, cheese, butter and meat. Also, if we had been lucky enough to trade a pair of gloves or socks with a trawler's cook, there would be a pot of jam.

All the tweeds made on St Kilda were one of three shades: light blue, light grey and brown. The brown is a colour derived from boiling stone moss and the resulting mixture was used as a dye, into which the wool was dipped until the tweed was the required reddish brown.

The kitchen in the house would be cleared of everything except chairs, which were set out in a circle. One person from each of the other families on the island would come and take his or her place in a chair. There would be anything up to twenty-five persons present including the grown up children of the family concerned, seated in the kitchen. The procedure involved went something like this. Each person was given a bundle of plain wool which was set beside him. Then he was given some dyed wool. The 'cards' were pieces of wood with short wire teeth like a brush and onto this you placed the white wool with some of the dyed wool. These were stroked between two cards until the required tone and colour of wool was achieved. It took about five minutes to complete one cardful of wool. The finished mixture was thrown in a heap on the floor. It started as a small hillock amassed in the centre, but eventually reached up to the ceiling. Carding would start around mid-day by the family themselves.

Around six o'clock the neighbours would start to appear one by one and carding would then go on till the early hours.

We children who were too young to card could only look on from the back and listen to the conversations, jokes and stories that were being told. Some of the stories had been handed down from ancient times; some concerned life on the mainland.

At one o'clock everybody stopped work for the night. The wool was stacked into canvas bags. The tables were brought back into the kitchen and laid out with a meal for all those who had taken part in the work. The highlight of the meal was a huge dumpling set in the middle of the table. Grace was said and the feasting then went on till around two a.m.

Another occasion I liked very much and which you might think very funny occurred when the tweed had to be taken down from the loft and washed. The tweed had to be washed because in order to weave the wool it had to be oiled so that the fibres held together during the weaving process. As everyone knows, oil is very difficult to wash off anything and it requires tremendous washing to extract it from thick tweed. The procedure used by the islanders to overcome this difficulty was carried out by the women. Half-a-dozen wooden tubs were placed in the middle of the kitchen floor. A huge boiling pot was suspended over a fire by a hook and chain hanging from the chimney. Into this pot was placed the next best thing to ammonia that the islanders could obtain. The pots under the beds were emptied each morning into a large barrel placed for strategic reasons behind the house. This fermenting liquid, which was up to a year old, was used to act as the detergent to shift the oil from the tweed. It was placed in the pot over the fire and brought to the boil. The boiling mixture was placed by the women – for this was woman's work – into the tubs. Washing soda and soft soap were added and the whole lot allowed to cool to a certain temperature. The smell was horrendous.

The women then tucked up their dresses to knee length and stepped into the tubs. They put as much tweed in as they required and began treading it very much in the fashion of treading grapes.

All the time they danced, they chanted some Gaelic rhythm, which I could never make out. Under the circumstances I never stayed around long enough to try to understand. They kept this activity going for ages, sweating, laughing and shouting until all the tweed had been through the tub.

When they had finished dancing in the tub the tweed was then spread across a long wooden table. Two women would get in each side of the table and pound the tweed for all they were worth. It was then thrown into the air to fall back onto the table. As this process was carried out, the tweed began to get thicker and thicker in texture. This action was called 'waulking' the tweed and was very arduous as the tweed was soaking wet. It was a great body exercise.

The tweed was then taken out to a running stream and my father and us boys went through the same process but with a certain relief that we were out in the open. Finally when the water was running clean and clear, the tweed was taken to a stone dyke. Here it was spread out and left to dry. When dried it was measured, rolled up and was now ready for selling.

Some of the Navy people would come up to the house when the women were treading the tubs as much in disbelief as curiosity. The women gave out loud shrieks and screamed at them to get out. They did not approve of strangers watching, especially with them showing bare knees, but it was all taken in good humour.

To visit the islets around St Kilda was every boy's dream, especially the Isle of Boreray. It had a magnetism all of its own. This probably arose due to the abundance of bird life to be found inhabiting the almost perpendicular rock. Every year the St Kildan men would send a party to shear the wild sheep which roamed freely over the craggy surface of Boreray. While there, the men would live for about fourteen days in underground houses which had been dug into the steep, sloping top of the islet. These had been built many years past in the bygone ages when the islanders had first visited the place and used it as a pasture for their sheep. On the occasion of every yearly visit the thick

Boreray in the distance – four miles from the main island
(Alasdair MacEachen)

undergrowth around the cleit-like houses had to be cleared away and the insides cleaned out to make them habitable.

I often visited Boreray on such an occasion. The puffins which covered the face of the island would come out of their burrows and stand at the entrance to their own underground homes. They would only fly off when you were so close that you felt you would be able to bend down and touch them. The birds took up their own hierarchy in their nesting habits. The gannets were on the high cliff tops and the fulmars on the cliff below them. Guillemots and razorbills were situated down on the ledges, and the kittiwakes screeching in and out of the caves produced the kind of music I loved to hear.

During their stay, the men lived off the rations they brought with them, and a sheep or two would be killed to supplement the diet. Of course, there were always seabirds in abundance to provide a square meal. The Sabbath was still observed as a day of rest and worship. All the men would gather in the largest of the underground houses and the service was held exactly as in the church on St Kilda.

Meanwhile the mothers took over the normal family worship each morning and night when the men folk were away.

It happened on one occasion when the men had visited Boreray that the dog of one of the villagers, which had been taken along for the trip, refused to leave with his master. No matter how they tried to cajole that dog it would run off as they approached him. Finally its owner despaired and the dog was left to its own devices. It would now have to fend for itself through the long winter months until the shearers returned the following year. When the St Kildans did return there, they found the dog in terrific condition. Its coat had a beautiful, glossy sheen and there was not an ounce of fat on the animal. It had lived off wild birds and the steep rocks had made the dog very fit and agile. Water had been got from the small well that opened from the ground and which provided the men with water during their stay. Although cautious and very wary at first, the dog finally took to the men again and this time returned with them to St Kilda when they left.

In 1917, the Government finally placed a large, naval gun on the island. The naval personnel often passed their time practising their firing, in case any enemy ship came to land. When they did fire, a terrific 'boom' reverberated throughout the hills. I was only nine years old when myself and two of my mates heard the crescendo of the first practice barrage. We had just been let out of school for a half-hour playtime. We thought our eardrums would explode and were thoroughly frightened. We ran for our lives towards home. Everyone from the village was outside their front doors, peering in the direction of the gun emplacement. Our parents spotted us running frantically towards them and immediately realised the cause of our terror. 'What are you running for?' they asked knowingly. With false courage we replied that we had come home for a piece of bread. 'But you never come home any other day for bread at this time,' my father stated. 'No,' I said, 'but today we are really hungry.' The villagers gathered round about laughing and we were quickly forgiven for our cowardice.

Chapter 6

The gun, installed on the island before the end of World War I
(Alasdair MacEachen)

As the days progressed we got used to the firing and the noise became a normal part of our daily life.

That big gun never fired a shell in anger. It was still there when in 1969 I visited the island with my eldest son, John. I related the story of how in my boyhood I had been frightened by its bark, as we leaned on its rusting hulk.

One morning just after World War I had commenced, we had gone outside our house to greet the new day when we noticed strangers coming towards our village from the hills in the distance. No one knew who they were but we were sure they were not military. An officer and four of the naval ratings went to meet them. The ratings carried their rifles just in case.

The strangers were thought to be Germans. We watched as the men were led two abreast through the village. They walked in silence and were thoroughly despondent. We later found out that they were all that was left of a Belgian crew who had been torpedoed by a German submarine the night before, just off Hirta. They had taken to the lifeboats and had just landed on the far end of the island. After a stiff climb they had scaled the cliffs before coming across a footpath which had led them to our village. The following day a British naval ship came to take them to the mainland.

I was sitting in class when Armistice Day, 11th November 1918, arrived. My teacher came in and told us to stand up and say a prayer. She told us the great news and led us in thanksgiving for our great deliverance. We were given the rest of the day off. We ran home in great jubilation, as much for having the time off as for the exciting news. The villagers were out celebrating and chatting excitedly. My parents were particularly excited, as probably all parents would be at the news which meant their sons would return. Sadness was intermixed with all the jubilation, for the news also meant that our friends the naval men and officers would now leave our island for good. It was truly a mixed blessing that the war had come to an end, although we never regretted the fact for one moment. In the four years that they had been stationed on Hirta, we had come to learn of the wondrous outside world and now we were once more to return to our isolation. These men had been wonderful to us children, teaching us to speak the English language, expanding our knowledge with stories of faraway places and giving us a wider perspective of the opportunities open to us elsewhere in the world. They had shown us such kindness as bringing us presents on their return from leave, holding parties for us at Christmas and generally showing great friendship. The older people, however, could not communicate with them very well because the aged St Kildans could only speak Gaelic, which was like a foreign language to all the naval men, except the two Lewismen. These latter two were, as a result, made especially welcome; even so, these two friends would now be returning to their own families.

The news of the Armistice, however, brought one matter to a head. Dick MacLean, one of the naval ratings, was married before he left to Mary MacDonald, one of the native girls.

Chapter 6

Everyone on the island was invited to the wedding and there was great merriment all round. At the great feast that followed the wedding there was a wedding cake that had been specially made in Glasgow. To finish off the treat there was jelly and fruit. We had never seen jelly before and its arrival caused quite a stir. I sat at the table with my father and an old gentleman who passed the remark, 'What in the world is this and how does one eat it? It's shaking all over.' After taking a spoonful he said, 'By Golly! It does taste nice, I think I shall have some more.' Navy rum was used to offer the toast while we children had mineral water, which tasted delicious.

At last the day arrived when the Navy had to leave. Many tears were shed as we made our farewells. This was especially so in the case of the young girls who had come to womanhood during the four years they were in our midst. A few of the departing men kept in touch with us by letter long after they left our shores. Some of these men retired ashore to work their own plots of land while others went back to sea. Only one ever returned to our isle; he had been a wireless operator during the duration and he returned as a tourist.

My brother arrived home six months after the war ended. He was made a 'Hero' having fought the Germans as a gunner in France and Gallipoli. He came through it without a scratch. Many a tale he told us of the war and his comrades who were killed in battle. John only stayed home for one year. He saw no future for him on the island and so he took a passage on a fishing trawler and went to Glasgow. My second oldest brother, Finlay, followed him the next year, and also went to Glasgow. Now there were only eight of the family left at home.

Chapter 7

In 1920, my sister Christine, who was only nine years old, died. She was a very religious child and grew up different from the rest of the family. She had a beautiful voice and was always singing religious hymns. Her favourite was 'Jesus loves me'. One Sunday night my mother stayed home to look after the five of us who were too young to go to the church. We all sat around the fireside while mother took out a Gaelic bible to read to us. As she read about the birth of baby Jesus and His life and why He was crucified, Christina burst into tears. My mother asked her why she was crying. 'Oh, because I love Him so much' was her reply. I said, 'You are a softy.' She turned to my mother and said, 'I am not a softy, I love Him more than anything else in this world.' She was more delicate than any of us but yet full of the joy of life, and played with us in and outside the house. She caught a chill one day and was confined to bed. It was winter time and our busy time of the year when the spinning and weaving was in progress and work went on till one and two in the morning.

We children went to bed at ten o'clock, because of school the following day. My father was weaving and mother and the two older sisters were spinning when they heard my sister, Christina, singing in the small bedroom off the kitchen. Mother told father to listen. 'Do you hear Christina singing? She must be feeling better as she was feverish earlier on in the night.' Father stopped to listen, and so did my sisters who were spinning; they thought it a bit strange. So mother got up and looked in the room, which was in semi-darkness. The singing stopped as she entered. Mother thought Christina must have gone to sleep so she returned to her spinning wheel and work continued. Then the singing started again so everyone stopped and listened. Mother felt a strange feeling come over her so she got up and went in, turned up the paraffin lamp and looked down on the bed. She gave a loud cry, shouting, 'Christina is dead; she looks so cold and serene, and very pale.'

The wailing and crying woke us up. Mother walked in and told us to get up, that our sister was dead. My brother and I could not believe it at first, but we got up and ran into the bedroom where she lay so very quiet. We bent over her and kissed her forehead, which was very cold, and then we all burst into tears; it all seemed so unreal. This was the first time I looked down on death and it was a fearful experience. When morning came and the village heard the sad news they came one after the other and joined in our bereavement. Earlier in the morning, whilst standing outside, I saw my father coming out of the house wringing his hands, tears running down his face, crying, 'Christina, Christina.' He walked past me and I saw him going into the byre. I followed him and listened; I heard him praying for strength and comfort, so I left and crept away quietly. I waited till he came out and he seemed much calmer, then he went back into the house.

When death came to anyone on the island, nobody did any kind of work for a whole week; everybody seemed to be sharing the same grief. Time is a great healer, and as the days and weeks went by we began to resume our normal way of life. Now there were only seven of the family at home.

More trawlers from Fleetwood, Hull and Aberdeen began calling on us. The Norwegian whalers also began to call, anchoring the whales they killed in the bay. The whaling factory was on West Loch Tarbert, owned by a Norwegian called Herlofsen. We used to visit those whalers when they came in, but the crew could only speak broken English, so we were at a disadvantage for carrying on any conversation with them. Sometimes when they brought in a freshly killed whale, they would cut out a large chunk of whale meat and say, 'Very good, very good, you eat.' We would shake our heads, signifying 'No, thank you.' When they had killed as many as six or seven whales they would lash them to the side of the ships and sail off to the factory. After they killed the first one or two whales they would leave them anchored in the bay. Sometimes a whole week would pass before they came back with the next two or three and they would then go away and hunt for more. If the weather was very warm, the whales' skin would peel off and hundreds of birds – gulls, fulmars, etc. – would swarm all over them. They also attracted many kinds of fish, which fed on the peeling skin. Their stomachs inflated out to look like a large red balloon. When this was pierced by a bird's beak the stench was vile and lingered over the whole bay for a long time. People in the village street often went around holding their noses after such an occurrence.

Eventually a ship would come and tow the whales to the processing plants. With five or six rotting carcasses lashed to the sides of the ship, it would return to Tarbert. What the smell must have been like for those on board the ship, in such close proximity to the rotting flesh, I hate to imagine.

My two eldest brothers left home and went to work in the shipyards in Glasgow. They met two Stornoway women and were married the same year. Work in Glasgow, though, was very difficult to come by in those days and eventually they had to return to the Isle of Lewis to try their luck in Stornoway itself. John found work in the herring processing industry, which was of considerable importance to the island economy. Finlay, my second brother, found a steady job in the gas works, a job he stayed in for a further six years.

My father would visit them every year, getting free passages on a trawler or a whaler visiting St Kilda. On one such occasion my father took time off to visit one of the naval men who had been stationed on our island during the war. The man was Kenneth MacLeod and he had since retired from the Navy to look after his croft.

My father was made very welcome during the visit, but his greatest surprise lay in store when after a few days Kenneth took him aside. Kenneth told my father that he was in love with my sister Annie and if he had no objections he would ask for her hand in marriage. My father was flabbergasted as he had no idea that such a love affair had been going on, although he knew Annie was receiving letters quite regularly. He told Kenneth that he had no objection, provided they were really in love. My father would ask Annie on his return whether she would like to marry this man. If Annie said yes, then my father would give them his blessing, for he knew Kenneth to be straight and honest and also a God-fearing man who was able to support her.

When father returned home he took Annie aside and with my mother present he put the question to her. 'Yes,' she said, 'I am in love with Kenneth but I will not marry him if either of you object.' They both agreed he was a good man and that they had no objection. When the family were told there were a few tears but also great joy.

Signal Staff, St Kilda Island, with Kenneth MacLeod in middle of back row (Christina MacQueen)

The following year father took Annie away on a whaler to get married in Stornoway. My mother could not go on such a long journey with all the rest of us children, so we remained at home. My two brothers were now able to represent Annie's relatives at the wedding.

On his return my father began to have thoughts about life on Hirta. There were now only five of us left at home and the family was getting smaller and smaller. He wondered whether to take all the family away and leave the island for good, but for the moment anyway, it was only a dream. Then another incident occurred, which this time involved Finlay John who was two years older than me.

My father was very friendly with a young engineer on one of the trawlers out of Fleetwood. This particular trawler often called in to the bay on its way to and from the fishing grounds around Rockall. The man was a Scot from Aberdeen and he always visited our house when ashore and he almost became one of the family. One day he asked whether he could give Finlay John a treat and take him on a trip to Fleetwood. Although wary about letting their son go, my parents eventually relented when told that they would return the very next trip. Both parents therefore agreed, but on the condition that the engineer took great care of Finlay John and with the proviso that they could not contribute anything to his expenses as money was scarce. The engineer told them that it was his pleasure for all the kindness shown to him in the past.

My brother, who was the toughest of all us boys (determination seemed to be his motto all his life), agreed to go. In fact he was thrilled to get away to see the world outside. As we watched the trawler leave the bay, we all wondered what his reaction would be to the unfamiliar surroundings.

The trawler was expected to return at the end of the week. One week, then two went past and still she did not return. By the third week there was still no sign of her and my parents were really worried for Finlay John's safety. The other islanders were also very anxious and every trawler that came into the bay was met with queries concerning the whereabouts of young Finlay. Eventually we found out that the trawler was now fishing different grounds. At last, a month since she left, the trawler was sighted streaming into the bay. We rowed out to where she lay at anchor and went aboard.

My father spoke to his friend. He was told that Finlay John was aboard another trawler, the *Caldew*, which was supposed to have returned him to St Kilda. The switch had taken place because that particular trawler had been fishing in the Minch between the mainland of Scotland and the Outer Isles on the last two trips at sea. My father was very annoyed with his friend for the lack of care and responsibility he had shown after the trust that had been placed in him.

A week later, the *Caldew* put into the harbour. Again Finlay John was not on board. The Captain assured my father that Finlay John was quite safe and that he had indeed been fishing with him not long since, but as he himself had had to fish in the Minch, Finlay John was put ashore in Fleetwood to arrange a lift with another trawler which was due to fish near our island. With that he handed over some toys and articles belonging to Finlay John.

When my mother was told the sorry tale and saw the belongings she was convinced her son had met with foul play. Under the circumstances, who could blame her in reaching such a conclusion? She said he must have drowned at sea and was most upset. Father decided to go to Fleetwood. He boarded a trawler, the *Lilly Melling*, which was returning with her catch. When the Captain heard my father's story he assured him he would help all he could. In fact he offered to allow my father to stay in his own home free of charge, until the whereabouts of Finlay John was discovered.

After reaching Fleetwood and discharging their catch they started making enquiries with the various companies to see if my brother was employed on their ships. At last my father found out that Finlay John had been taken on as a member of the crew of a small fishing boat. After further enquiries he found out that this

Finlay John, on the right (Christina MacQueen)

particular ship was away at sea and was not due to return till the following week.

When the boat finally pulled into port my father was standing on the quay waiting. He walked back to where the boat had tied up to unload. There was Finlay John, oblivious to all the worry he had caused. At first he did not want to return as he rather liked the life at sea. Father, on the other hand, would have none of this and told him he was too young to be left behind. Finlay John was paid off, the princely sum of £2, plus a percentage of the catch.

My father returned and thanked the Captain who had been so hospitable and allowed him to stay in his home. Then the two of them made a few purchases to take back and found a trawler which was going near St Kilda and which would take them home. My father never forgave his friend for the way he let him down.

Years later Finlay John did return to the sea when he became a Merchant Seaman. His ship was torpedoed in the Atlantic by a German submarine on the first day after World War II was declared and he spent the duration as a prisoner of war.

Chapter 8

In 1924[1] my father decided we would leave the island for good. He had suffered from asthma for many years and only seemed to find relief from it when he was on trips away from St Kilda. My brothers, who lived in Stornoway, told him that he would be able to work without the hardship and stress that living on Hirta entailed.

At that time Lord Leverhulme, the founder of Sunlight, owned the islands of Lewis and Harris. He was a millionaire industrialist and had plans to develop the islands. This plan entailed the building of houses for the workers and expansion of the town of Stornoway. The port facilities of Stornoway were to be developed so that it could cater for a large fishing industry, and act as a fishing terminal for factories, which would provide employment for the natives of the islands. The whole scheme was a token of gratitude from Leverhulme for the contributions and sacrifices the Scots had made in helping to defeat the Germans in the 1914–1918 war.

However, the returning soldiers and sailors did not want or approve of the scheme. All they required was a piece of land of their own on which they could build a home, keep cattle and develop as they wished. Lord Leverhulme, realising he could not pacify the islanders, transferred the scheme to Obbe in Harris. On the whole the new site was less favourable to develop. The name of part of Obbe was eventually changed to Leverburgh.

[1] The veracity of this date is questionable; it may have been 1922.

Chapter 8

Lord Leverhulme was living in Stornoway Castle which was within a mile of my brother's house. During one of my father's annual visits to Stornoway he was persuaded to seek an interview with this great industrialist. He got in touch with Lord Leverhulme's secretary and the interview was arranged.

The meeting took place in the Castle. His Lordship listened to my father's reason for wanting to leave the island. Lord Leverhulme was especially interested in the fact that my father's asthma attacks improved when he left the island. Lord Leverhulme explained that he too suffered badly from this illness and told my father he had his sympathy. 'Yes, I will be able to help you,' he said. 'You bring your wife and four children and anyone else who wishes to leave the island. I personally guarantee you all work and eventually a real home. In the meantime until such houses can be provided, you can all live in a large temporary house. I shall get in touch with my Manager in Leverburgh and arrange everything for your arrival.' The interview ended.

My father now made up his mind that he would leave the island the following autumn. On his arrival back in St Kilda he told the family his intention. We were highly delighted that we would all leave as one family. The islanders, though, were rather sad that here was one house that would close its doors for ever. Some of the younger people already knew that our way of life in St Kilda was doomed. Their future lay outside those shores. Since the war six men and two women had left for other lands and without young people life was bound to come to a standstill. Now, three more young men said they would also come away with us and seek work in Leverburgh.

In the spring of 1924 (*see note opposite*) my father left to take up employment as a labourer in Leverburgh. He was going to work a preliminary three months to earn enough money before evacuating us from the island. He returned in August to collect us and pack our household belongings. There was not much in the way of packing to be done though, as we possessed little in this line. Most of our furniture was homemade and only suitable for our spartan way of life. My father arranged with some friends who lived in Tarbert on the Isle of Harris that some of the family would travel in advance. The rest of the family would follow in one of the whalers a week later. The first party to leave consisted of my sister Mary, one of the other islanders and myself. On the morning of our departure most of the islanders gathered on the small quay. Some were weeping and looking rather sad. At that time I was only sixteen years old. My uncle, who had delivered me into the world, pressed four shillings into my hand as he bade me goodbye. My aunt gave me five shillings and my father ten shillings. This money was to be used to provide for my keep until we met up again in one week's time.

The young lads who I had grown up with told me to be sure and ask the whaler's Captain to let me pull on the ship's siren. When we had said our last goodbye we put on board. Four dead whales were lashed to the side of the ship and two were towed astern as

The family home, House No. 3, second from the left (now houses the St Kilda Museum) (Alasdair MacEachen)

we made our un-dramatic exit from St Kilda bay. I went to see the Captain and found that he could not speak any English. So I made a sign and simulated pulling the ship's siren. He nodded his head in agreement. I pulled and pulled for ten minutes until we were out of sight of the bay. The Captain made a sign, as much as to say, enough. So I left the bridge. As we slowly sailed on, the coastline of St Kilda and the other islets became hazy in the distance astern. There was a heavy swell and a sea haze hung over the waters. Eventually we lost sight of our island home and we were alone in miles and miles of ocean. All we could hear was the throbbing of the ship's engines as it cut laboriously through the waves. Most of the crew had gone to sleep in their cabins. We were invited to use the dining room if we required to lie down. This invitation was accepted by my sister who was feeling a bit sea sick.

I stayed on deck for a little while, not feeling very happy and wishing I had never left home. Still, some of my friends, the gulls and fulmars, were escorting us. I watched their aerial ballet. Every now and again they would land on the towed carcasses and peck at the skins. I envied them their wings and the freedom they had to return to my beloved island.

It took ten hours to arrive at the Isle of Harris. As we drew near my sister and my friend Donald came up from below deck. We were offered food but none of us felt hungry. It was the first time we had been on such a journey by sea. The smell of the ship and the rotting whales did not help our appetites.

As we sailed into West Loch Tarbert, towards the whaling station, the stench became unbearable. Men were everywhere busy cutting huge strips off the dead whales. Steam and smoke rose high in the air from the oil extraction processes. The harbour was a hubbub of activity. The whales that we had towed were anchored near the pier. The ship itself was then tied up to the pier. We bid the Captain and crew goodbye.

A native of Harris stepped forward. He greeted us and said he had expected us. We were to stay out at his house, as had been arranged. He took us to his home and made us very welcome.

After tea, which we now enjoyed, we felt a little more cheerful. Before retiring this man and his family held worship, in which we joined. We were then taken to our separate rooms. We did not have much baggage. My sister carried a small case, Donald had a small bag and I had all that I was standing in.

The following day we went by bus to Tarbert and for the first time in our lives we did some shopping. We were amazed to see how men travelled on a two wheel bicycle and could not understand how they did not fall off. The fare on the bus was one shilling for a journey of four miles. We began to realise that we could not get very far without money. Everything that we fancied in the shops was also costing money. This resulted in us taking great care of the little pocket money we did have, so instead of taking the bus back to our friends' home, we walked. Looking back now, I think that the wear on our shoes was probably just as costly as the shilling we saved.

The next day we were to separate. My sister was to go to Stornoway and my friend Donald MacDonald was to leave for Leverburgh to look for employment with Lord Leverhulme. I was supposed to stay till the following week when my father would arrive with the rest of the family. The separation was too much for me and to be left behind with strangers was unbearable. My sister boarded the bus and set off on her journey to our brother's house in Stornoway. I made up my mind to stick with my friend Donald and told our Harris friend of my decision. 'Well,' he said, 'I cannot hold you against your will, but your father will be annoyed.'

That evening we boarded the mail boat which took us to Rodel. After a short journey we disembarked and set off by foot on the four mile walk to Leverburgh. It was getting quite dark and night was fast descending when a lorry pulled up alongside us. The driver asked where we were headed and I told him Leverburgh. 'Right, jump in the back and I will take you,' he said. This we did and were soon travelling up the glen towards our destination. The road climbed steeply until finally we began to descend a very steep road indeed. Suddenly there was a thud. The lorry hit a car which was coming up the road in the opposite direction. As the lorry jerked to a halt we jumped out, rather shaken but none the worse for wear. Both drivers were arguing very heatedly. We made sure that no one was hurt. My friend turned to me and whispered, 'Let's away from here, otherwise the police will come and we will have to go to court.' This was rather a frightening prospect we wanted to avoid at all costs. We were unduly frightened of being questioned by the police. We left the bickering drivers and walked the rest of the way to Leverburgh.

We were to look for a building called 'Bridge House' which was situated near the river. This house had been used by many St Kildans who had been visiting in the area. They had always been made very welcome and the lodgings were clean and comfortable. We found the house, knocked and went in. The house was owned by an old woman who resided there with her married son. The son had been married less than two years and apart from his wife, the other occupants of the house were a set of twins in a cradle.

Conversation revolved around the various St Kildans who had stayed from time to time in their abode. They knew my father well as he had lodged with them during the summer. I explained why I was there instead of stopping in Tarbert. They said that they understood and I was not to worry. They would take care of me until my father arrived.

In the meantime I was to help the young mother by looking after the twins while she went out to milk the cows. I would also have to draw the water from the well and generally make myself useful round the house. I agreed to do this as I did not have too much money to otherwise pay my way. We were then shown up to our room in the attic which was small but comfortable.

Next morning Donald went off to look for work. He succeeded and was employed as a labourer in a quarry, working for a rate of 4p an hour. The hours were from eight a.m. until five-thirty p.m. and Saturday work finished at noon. He would begin the following Monday.

Towards the end of the week I received a letter from my father. He would be arriving early Monday morning. I was delighted. They were due to arrive on the *Dunara Castle* at Leverburgh. Early Monday morning I got up before the rest of the household and made my way towards the pier. The *Dunara Castle* anchored in the sound and small boats plied their way to and from her in order to bring her cargo ashore. When the first boat returned I enquired of one boatman if my family was on board. 'No,' he said. The ship had not called at Tarbert before coming to Leverburgh so no passengers had been picked up. I felt very disappointed as I walked back to the house. I arrived about lunchtime and was met by Donald. 'Has your family arrived?' he said. 'No,' I said, 'they must be coming by road.' 'Well, I do not know what will happen to you in the meantime,' he said. I enquired what he meant. 'The lady of the house is very annoyed at you for not staying to look after the children. She told me that you need not come back as she will not give you a meal.' I was flabbergasted and by now thoroughly depressed. There was nothing left for me to do but turn around and return to the pier. I asked a boatman if he would take me out to the *Dunara Castle* so that I could return to Tarbert. There I hoped to find a whaler that would take me back to St Kilda. The boatman agreed to take me to the ship lying out in the sound so I bade Donald farewell.

I paid 23p to the Purser for the single fare to Tarbert. On board I met another young St Kildan who was going to Glasgow where his brother was working. It was a great surprise to both of us to meet this way. I had not eaten all day and was famished. We went to see the steward who in turn gave us a mug of tea and some sandwiches, for which he charged us 10p. It took us two hours to make the trip from Leverburgh to Tarbert.

We pulled into the quay, where I was very fortunate indeed. Who should be standing there but my father and brother? 'Where on earth do you think you are going?' my father shouted. I could hardly believe my ears. I told him I was on my way back to St Kilda. Donald Hugh, who I had met up with on board said, 'Are you going to Glasgow?' to which I told him, 'No.' 'Did you get my letter saying I would be in Leverburgh on Monday?' my father asked. 'Yes, but seeing the *Dunara Castle* did not call in here to pick up passengers I thought that you had not left St Kilda yet,' I answered. 'No,' he said, 'we came over on a whaler earlier than expected but the ship never called in to pick us up. I have now hired a lorry and everything is piled up on it. Your mother and sisters are waiting beside it. It's lucky for you that we stopped a few minutes to watch the *Dunara Castle* dock, otherwise we would have been on our way and you would have missed us.' My father then turned to Donald Hugh and said to him, 'What about you joining us? There is plenty of employment in Leverburgh. Besides, your uncle Donald is here with us and he is going to stay with us when we reach Leverburgh.'

I met my mother and the rest of the family and then told them what had happened. My father was very annoyed that I had been treated so unkindly; still, we ceased to worry about that as we all piled into the lorry. Off we went on our overland journey.

It was well after midnight when we reached the hut that was to be our home for the next two years. There was no electricity, so light was provided by candles. We were unable to light the paraffin lamps we brought from St Kilda because we had not taken any paraffin on such a journey. We unpacked our bedding and took some food out and mother prepared a meal. After we had eaten, we gathered around and in the dim candle light we said our thanksgiving. Prayers that night were kept short as everyone was thoroughly tired from the arduous journey.

The rest of the week was spent organising our new home. Our furniture consisted of four bunk beds, a double bed and one single bed; there was a long table and three long seats made of wood; last but not least was the stove. Outside in another hut was the toilet and washroom. The interior of our hut was divided into separate rooms by hanging sheets from wall to wall. This provided scant but extra privacy. Our living conditions were now less favourable than those we had left on St Kilda but this we hoped would soon be corrected after we had settled into the run of things. Mother took my younger sisters along to enrol at the local school and my father, brothers and myself went along to the employment office to sign on for work. We were not kept waiting long. The following Monday morning at eight o'clock sharp we were to report to different quarries. There we were to work as navvy labourers. So we returned home for the short while until our employment was to begin.

Monday came and we reported as instructed to the various quarries. I remember the picture of utter confusion that first struck me. There were hundreds of men scattered far and wide, drilling, digging, blasting, levelling and pushing barrows. This particular area was to be the site for houses that would eventually be built, another quarry was preparing the site for a factory and so the jigsaw was forming. Our wages were 4p an hour and for that we sweated and laboured all day. We were happy, though, because this was our first employment and we were glad of it. The whole project was, as I said before, to make Leverburgh into a fishing port. New piers were being erected on the water's edge to accommodate the ships and fishing boats that were expected. I found the life very tough and some of the navvies even tougher. I was introduced to language I had never heard before in my life.

Luck was to come my way, though, and I was saved from the road that my life had seemed to have turned down. A local shopkeeper named Lowe came up to my father, who he knew very well as a customer, and took him aside. 'Listen,' he said, 'your son is not the type to work in these conditions, he can do much better. With your approval I will offer him a job as my assistant. Although the wages will not be as high as he is earning now, it will be a cleaner and better life and I will personally train him. What do you say?' My father said, 'I will put your proposal to Calum and if he agrees and cares for such a life, I will not stand in his way.'

So I changed my employment to that of shop assistant in a general merchandise shop. My new boss taught me how to sell to the customers, give the correct change and memorise the price of goods. I picked up the trade quickly and was soon left in charge of the shop. My wages were £1.75 per week. I worked from nine a.m. till eight p.m. when the shop closed for the night. After this it was my job to take the post, which had been left in the shop, to the Post Office, a round trip of three miles, before I was allowed to return home. This was accepted as being all part of a day's work.

My parents found it hard to make ends meet with such a large and young family as we required a lot of feeding and clothing. I handed over my pay each Saturday and was given back 25p as pocket money. After a year we were all feeling disillusioned with the way things had turned out and realised we were better off living on our own island. My brother and Donald Hugh made up their minds that they would go to Glasgow to work in the shipyards. They expected to earn more money there than in the quarries of Leverburgh. My father took an extra job as part-time night-watchman to make a little extra on top of the money he got for working all day. Eventually, though, his health began to suffer. This is how we carried on until the following summer. It was at this time that we heard that Lord Leverhulme was dying and rumours began to spread that the whole Leverburgh project would cease. My father was very worried about the consequences to our family if this was to occur. We would probably have to return to St Kilda.

We were told of the tragic news of Lord Leverhulme's death soon afterwards. Work came to a standstill and all the men were paid off. It was a disaster for many families. One could hardly believe the hardship which this created. The place looked desolate – you would never believe that only a few months before it had been a hive of activity. My family was forced to pack up and leave for Stornoway. There we hoped to live with my brother's family and Annie and her husband until my father and I could find some work. Our hopes and aspirations were dashed when the life left Lord Leverhulme's body.

My eldest brother, John, was living at that time in a one-room flat with his wife and three children. Finlay, my second eldest brother, had a three-bedroom house but as well as his own twin children he had his mother-in-law and brother-in-law living in the house. Annie lived out in the country with her husband and his parents. They were in the process of building their own house on the croft. We therefore had to stay at Finlay's. We slept like sardines for the first two nights. After that my parents took my three younger sisters to the country to stay with Annie. I stayed on at Finlay's in case I could find work in the town.

Soon after my father arrived at Annie's, he became ill. His health was very run down. My sister's mother-in-law wondered why my father went down every day to the seashore. She had known my father many years now and thought this strange. One day she followed him very quietly and hid herself behind a boulder. Then she heard my father praying. She was amazed and only now realised that this was the vigil he kept every day. She listened as he prayed to God for comfort and strength for the island of St Kilda and its people. She felt ashamed of eavesdropping on such a good living man in his hour of agony. My father died a few days later.

CERTIFICATE OF DEATH.

WIDOWS ORPHANS AND OLD AGE CONTRIBUTORY PENSIONS ACTS, 1925 and 1929.

Name and Surname, &c. [Give contents of Col. (1) of Entry]	William MacDonald Labourer & Crofter Married to Ann MacQueen
When and where died	1925 October Fourth 5 Lundale Uig usual Residence St-Kilda
Age 51 years	

I hereby certify that the above particulars are extracted by me from Entry No. 11 in the Register Book of Deaths pertaining to the District of Uig in the County of Ross for the year 1925

15th September 1924 M. Macrae Registrar.

(Date)

Death certificate of William MacDonald (Calum's father)
(John MacDonald)

Chapter 8

This story only came to light after my father's death, when the old lady told my sister. My mother was now in a dreadful state with three young girls to support and I was still without work. She received a widow's pension of 75p and this was all the money that was coming into the family. My brothers helped as much as they could, even though they had families of their own to support. I used to go to the gasworks where Finlay was the fireman. The gasworks was situated near a kippering shed where herring was smoked. The air round this area always had an odour that was strange, but bearable.

My brother told the boss of the kippering shed our family situation and how I had been unable to find work since arriving in Stornoway. This man made a fine gesture and said I could start work with his nightshift man, starting the following nightshift and the wages were £2 per week.

My first job since we left Leverburgh; even though it was only seasonal work it was great to get some work to help mother and my sisters. When the season was over, the manager of the gasworks noticed how I was always there helping my brother firing the retorts which produced the gas. He asked me if I cared for a job painting the windows of his house and doing odd jobs in the Gas House. I said, 'Yes, I do not mind what kind of work as long as I have got a job.' He engaged me on the spot.

My brother and another man were the firemen. One undertook the nightshift and the other the dayshift. These roles were reversed every week. The hours were from eight a.m. to six p.m. When you started the nightshift the change over took place on a Sunday. From eight o'clock on Sunday morning till six o'clock on Monday morning, you had a whole day's rest. The wages were 50p a shift. It so happened that my brother's mate was taken seriously ill and I was asked to take over as fireman. It was a hard, hot life. One needed a lot of stamina to cope with the heat of the furnaces; you sweated most of the time, especially in the winter, for the town of Stornoway completely depended on gas for heat and light. The furnaces were fired twice in the shift, which meant twenty-eight times a week. Besides firing the furnaces I had to go underground and clean the furnaces, which in turn fired the retorts. It was also part of my job to clean out the purifiers once a week. One had to work very hard to maintain the plant and keep it working to its full capacity in order to keep the town well supplied with gas.

Life seemed to be improving for the family now. I had a steady job and we had a council home of our own for the first time. In 1928 my sister Mary met Alex MacLeod, who had been a naval officer on our island during the war. He was home on leave from sea. They fell in love and married in Inverness. He returned to sea a year later when their first child had been born. He was sailing out to Australia and soon sent for his wife and child to come to settle in Melbourne. This was another break in the family and a sad departure when she emigrated. It was forty years before I was to see her again, by which time my mother and my eldest brother would be dead and her husband also passed on. She married again, this time to an Australian by the name of Joe Hill. They both came over again in 1974 for a two month visit; it was a great get-together occasion for the family. She was seventy-two years old and still had her St Kilda accent and the same charm she had when she lived on the island.

However, I am digressing and will return to my story.

Chapter 9

In 1929 I made a return visit to St Kilda. It was my first visit to my island home since I had left in 1924. I still had uncles and aunts living there, but life was changing and dying. Most of the young men were after leaving the island. The elderly realised that without the young the old could not maintain their ancient traditional way of living.

A petition was raised asking the Government of the day to help the St Kildans to move to the mainland of Scotland. This, together with a national press campaign, persuaded the Government to grant their request. In my view the course they decided upon was tragic in its consequences. The families who had for generations lived as one community were scattered far and wide and not kept together as a unit. Many of the older folk were broken hearted because they now found themselves uprooted and set down among strangers. Often these people spoke in a different tongue to the St Kildans and the elders would never be able to communicate. They were sentenced to a life of loneliness merely because no one had the foresight to keep the community intact – or was it the extra cost this would have incurred? Happiness for these people was forsaken for the sake of expedience.

At the time of the evacuation in 1930 there were fifty-six native-born islanders alive; today in the year 1976 there are only twenty-four natives of St Kilda still alive. Our descendants, whose numbers are in the hundreds, are dispersed throughout the world and to them St Kilda is a word of mouth memory handed down to them by their parents.

After a dispute with the manager of the gasworks I left his employ and was engaged in building the first power station in the town. My first work was helping with the laying of electric cables underground throughout the town. This was work which did not last long, however. Once all the cables had been installed and the electric power initiated, I was paid off and joined the unemployed queues for the first time. I received 75p per week.

My prospects had taken a turn for the worst. Two months of being on the dole passed and still no work was forthcoming. I was beginning to get very apprehensive when I received a letter from A.G. Ferguson, the St Kildan tweed merchant in Glasgow. He asked me if I would care to join him on a visit to St Kilda. The purpose of this visit was to catch wild sheep on the island of Soay. These would then be transferred to the main island of Hirta.

The SS Hebrides *was introduced to the St Kilda passage in the summer of 1898, transporting locals, visitors and goods between St Kilda and the mainland. It was in 1929, the year of Calum's visit, that John McCallum (owner of the* Hebrides*) and Martin Orme (owner of the* Dunara Castle*) amalgamated to form the McCallum Orme & Co. Ltd shipping company* (Christina MacQueen)

A.G. Ferguson (Neil Ferguson)

The ownership of the islands had now passed from the hands of MacLeod of MacLeod who had owned the islands until the evacuation, to Lord Dumfries who now instigated the trip.

I grasped at this opportunity and accepted the kind offer by return of post. So in June 1932 I joined the *SS Hebrides* which was lying at anchor in the Sound of Harris. This ship made annual voyages every year to the Western Isles. On board was A.G. Ferguson, his brother Neil and his wife Annie, who in turn was my aunt. Their son Donald John was with them, as was Finlay MacQueen (an uncle), Finlay Gillies, Donald MacDonald, John and his brother Neil Gillies and their sister-in-law, Kirsty Gillies. It was quite a meeting, for we had not seen each other for many years. We were all terribly excited to be going back to our dear island for the duration of that summer. We headed out of the

Neil Ferguson back on St Kilda, standing outside the family home at No. 5 with St Kilda Post Office adjoining house (Neil Ferguson)

Sound of Harris at two p.m. and arrived in St Kilda at seven the same evening. There was great activity getting our stores ashore via the ship's small boat. This task was not finally completed until well after midnight. The ship anchored in the bay till the following noon. In the meantime the passengers who had landed with us the previous night embarked early in the morning.

All through the night my aunt and I cleaned out the old homestead and unpacked the stores. When the ship left we gathered together to plan our stay.

A.G. Ferguson, who had a boat stowed away on the island, suggested we got her ready to visit the islets. It was like old times with everybody so happy to be back. We caught a hundred wild Soay sheep and transferred them to the main island, and killed three for our own use. In our spare time we wove tweed for A.G. Ferguson who had brought the yarn ready for the loom. This was the first time I ever sat on a loom weaving and as I was going to be paid for this trip, all my free time was spent weaving. We feasted on puffins and fulmars like the olden days. Everyone slept in their old homes except for me, as my aunt would not let me sleep in my father's home. Instead I had to sleep in her home. She told me on several occasions during these days, 'I wish we had never left here. Today I feel so happy, as if I had never left here.'

At last our stay was near an end and the ship was due to arrive. We packed to leave, with each of us to go our separate ways. We went to the church for the last service together; the sermon was taken over by my aunt's husband, Neil, who was an elder of the church. It was said in Gaelic.

Finlay MacQueen back on St Kilda (Neil Ferguson)

Looking over the cemetery wall towards Dun
(Alasdair MacEachen)

Neil talked of the past and of the Christians lying at rest in the quiet burial ground behind the village. Knowing that none of us present at that moment would ever lie beside them, it was a sad service but so very true of the people who had lived from generation to generation in a world of their own making.

The *SS Hebrides* arrived and passengers came ashore. They walked up and down the village before returning to the ship. We also went on board with them. I landed in Harris and made my way to Stornoway while the rest of the party carried on to Glasgow before separating. For my part of the expedition and working on the islands I received a cheque for £20 from A.G. Ferguson with all expenses paid.

For the rest of the year I did any sort of work that came to hand, such as discharging boats of coal and fishing drifters; also taking patients out to the Inverness psychiatric hospital. These were not very pleasant jobs, but jobs that nevertheless needed to be done.

Chapter 9

In 1933 A.G. Ferguson wrote to me again, asking if I would join a party to St Kilda. This time Lord Dumfries and his party were going to visit his newly acquired possession, which was to be a bird sanctuary. A.G. Ferguson pointed out that I would be a great asset, being young and able to show them around the island. The *SS Dunara Castle* picked me up in the Sound of Harris, like the year before. On board were Lord and Lady Dumfries, the Hon. Bob and Willie Stirling from Keir House, Stirling, Lord David Crichton Stuart and Mr John Drummond.

Lord David Stuart on St Kilda (Neil Ferguson)

They went to some of the other islands and in the *Caithmor* at night we caught two shearwaters, ringed them and then let them fly away again. We also ringed some puffins and fulmars. They were much impressed with the whole trip and in 1936 made another one. We, the natives, stayed on for a month roaming about the island, lobster fishing and sea fishing, feeling much at home like the old days.

Chapter 10

Soon after returning to Stornoway I received another letter from A.G. Ferguson, this time asking me if I cared to join Lord Dumfries's staff, at Dumfries House, Old Cumnock. His Lordship was very much impressed with me while we were on St Kilda. He said he would like to help me, if I were still unemployed, by employing me as an odd job man while I was gaining experience for a better situation in the household staff. My wages were to be

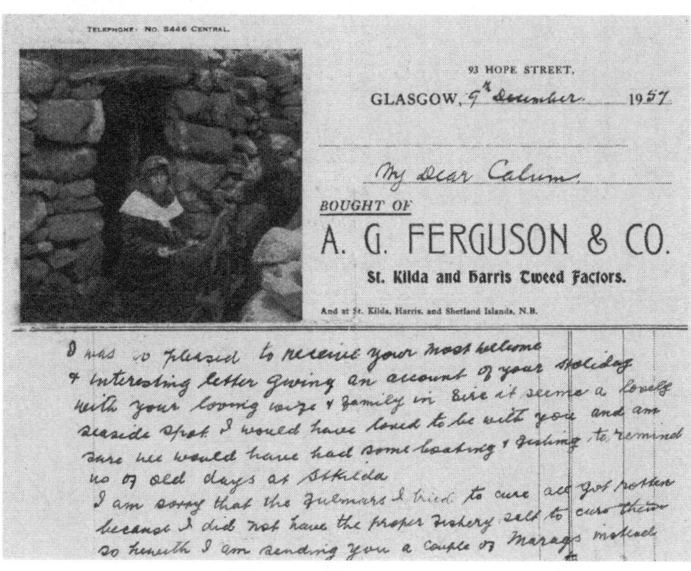

TELEPHONE: NO. 5446 CENTRAL.

93 HOPE STREET,

GLASGOW, 9th December 1957.

My Dear Calum,

BOUGHT OF

A. G. FERGUSON & CO.

St. Kilda and Harris Tweed Factors.

And at St. Kilda, Harris, and Shetland Islands, N.B.

I was so pleased to receive your most welcome
& interesting letter giving an account of your holiday
with your loving wife & family in Eire it seems a lovely
seaside spot. I would have loved to be with you and am
sure we would have had some boating & fishing, to remind
us of old days at St Kilda
I am sorry that the fulmars I tried to cure all got rotten
because I did not have the proper fishery salt to cure them
so herewith I am sending you a couple of Maraggs instead

A letter to Calum from A.G. Ferguson (John MacDonald)

£1 all found after takings, and after talking it over with my mother and family I decided I would give it a try and wrote accepting the situation. I duly arrived a week later at Dumfries House and was introduced to the housekeeper, butler and the rest of the staff. The following day I was confronted by His Lordship and Her Ladyship who heartily welcomed me as a member of their staff. This, my first introduction to the elite, was quite an occasion. The butler informed me of the duties I was required to carry out. My day started at six-thirty a.m. and I had to stoke the domestic boilers, sweep the whole corridors (and scrub and wash on my knees said corridors once a week) and carry coals in the buckets to the rooms, some three flights up, as well as give a hand washing up in the pantry after meals; also wash the servants' dishes, look after a small aviary outside and brush down the front steps every day. There was a break for rest from two p.m. till six p.m. every day and then work continued till eleven p.m. after the dinner dishes had been washed. There was also one day off a week. Included in the large sum of £1 a week, there was an allowance of 17p for laundry and 2p a day for beer. I was also allowed one suit made to measure, valued at not more than £12 a year, plus a pair of dungarees for working in. After a week I began to wonder if I had taken leave of my senses, but gradually as I came to know the rest of the staff I began to enjoy the life.

There was much entertaining of the gentry and house parties were held frequently. The staff consisted of the butler, the head housekeeper, a footman, a pantryman (oddman), three maids, one chef, three kitchen hands and a nanny, plus a maid and two grooms for Her Ladyship, who did a lot of horse-riding. We, the staff, made our own entertainment and amusements which were mostly playing cards, listening to gramophone records and an occasional flutter on the horse races. This was my first initiation into gambling. The butler and chef were having a 'flutter' on a horse daily. I was told to try my luck on 3 x 6*d.* doubles win, but I seldom won. However, I never forgot to send my mother £3 per month for she always came first. I soon realised I had become the staff 'bookie' and that I could make more money from this than from gambling. Within a fortnight I was up more than £24, mostly from the butler and chef, until one day the chef won after having a treble up and I had to pay £20.50, so I quickly retired from the business as bookie, but it was fun while it lasted.

After two years I decided to leave private service and go to Glasgow, to see if I could find a better-paying job. I asked the butler to inform His Lordship I was giving a month's notice. Later in the evening His Lordship called me to the drawing room. I entered, bowed to him, then stood to attention. He said, 'MacDonald, is it true you have given notice to my butler, Jim Alison, that you are leaving?' 'Yes, my Lord,' I said. 'Will you tell me why? Are you not happy here?' 'Oh yes, my Lord,' I said, 'but I find I cannot support myself and my mother and two sisters on my wage here. I therefore decided to go and look for a job where I can earn more and be able to support them.' His Lordship replied, 'MacDonald, I don't want to lose you and especially since you are a St Kildan, for I intend to visit your island again from time to time and I would like to take you with me. Would you think it over if I made you my personal valet and footman? I feel I need a second footman as we entertain a lot. Besides, you would be looking after some of my guests, unpacking when they arrive. I will raise your wages to £1.25 a week, plus you will be receiving tips from the guests you look after, which will greatly increase your wages from what you are earning now.' I considered His Lordship's offer there and then and replied, 'I will accept your Lordship's offer, but I have no experience in valeting.' His Lordship smiled and said, 'Don't worry, I will get the butler to teach you. I am sure you will find it easy and I am pleased you will stay with me. I shall tell my butler to get you measured for a footman's uniform. He will also teach you how to lay out my clothes in the morning and for the evening meal.'

This for me was a step up the ladder upon which I would come into contact with the nobility, through offering them my personal service. My jobs now included laying out the dining table, serving meals and pouring out various wines.

When the Dumfries's entertained, it was a very lavish affair. It was fascinating to stand back and listen to their conversations and after dinner jokes. During these occasions I had to step over and remove each guest's plate as he or she finished each course. I had then to wait for all the guests to finish before serving another course. Dinner often consisted of as many as five courses and some very exotic dishes came from the kitchen of the French chef. I often wondered how they never complained of indigestion, so different were the dishes to the ones served to the staff downstairs and even more different to the salt mutton and fulmar we used to eat on Hirta, which was washed down with a glass of fresh spring water. I wonder which was more beneficial to the body.

Lord and Lady Dumfries had twin sons who were about one year old when I joined the staff. One was Lord John, the other Lord David and they were lovely boys. I became very fond of them, and sometimes I used to go and watch their nanny getting them ready for bed. They were very natural, like all boys of their age, and full of fun. Later Lord James was born and later still Lady Fiona, who was my favourite as she was so beautiful and sweet.

I stayed with the family for four years and in that time I met many of the nobility who came to the grouse and pheasant shootings. I used to travel with His Lordship as his 'gun-loader', out on the moors. It was a great life and experience for me. Our shooting parties often consisted of such gentry as the Duke of Montrose, Lord Mansfield, the Hon. Drummond-Hay, the Hon. Boland, the Hon. W. Stirling, Lord Robert David Rheadian, brother of Lord Dumfries and Lord Forbes, as well as many other rich and famous people. Yet however much one mixed with them and spoke with them, one was aware that one was only a servant. There is always a barrier between the rich and the poor, which to my way of thinking is quite wrong; for without the poor they would never be rich and I believe that on this earth we are all equal in the sight of God.

The Butes owned a large estate which consisted of the island of Bute on the Clyde, where they had Kames Castle and Mount

Stuart; a large house in Charlotte Square, Edinburgh; Old Cumnock (where Dumfries House stands) and Cardiff Castle, as well as other estates in Wigtownshire, if I remember correctly. And yet with all their wealth, their staff were living on pennies, when one considered the long hours we worked, from early morning till late at night.

In 1937, if my memory serves me correctly, His Lordship told me he was going to take a party to my island home and he would take me and one of his kitchen hands to look after his party. I was delighted by this news and by the thought of a visit to my beloved Hirta once again. Also on the trip were to be some of my fellow St Kildans. It was arranged that I should first take my annual holiday at home in Stornoway. The party was travelling from Glasgow on the *SS Hebrides* and I was to travel from Stornoway to Leverburgh and pick up the ship in the Sound of Harris.

I spent my fortnight's holiday with my family in Stornoway and returned from there to Leverburgh by bus to await the *SS Hebrides.* I stayed with friends I had come to know when I first left St Kilda to work for Lord Leverhulme in 1924. They lived in a blackhouse (or thatched roof cottage) close to the shore. Nearby was a waterfall. I received a telegram from Lochmaddy, saying the *SS Hebrides* would stop in the Sound of Harris the following day to pick me up.

Unfortunately for me, everyone in the house slept so soundly that night that none of us heard the ship's siren sounding for four hours, as the waterfall drowned the sound. When I eventually woke up and looked out of the window she was after heaving anchor and passing through the channel into the Atlantic, on the way to St Kilda.

I was flabbergasted, knowing His Lordship depended on me to look after the party and now there was no way to get to the island. I felt dismal and thought, this will mean the sack and discharge from His Lordship's service. I got a bus back to Stornoway where all the family wondered what had happened to me. When I told them, they were very sympathetic. They also could not see how I was to get to the island – until I met my eldest brother, John. He said he thought there was a fishing trawler from Aberdeen taking on fresh water at the pier, and so we went down to see if they were fishing near St Kilda.

We met the Captain and explained my predicament to him. 'Yes,' he said, 'I am going to Rockall and will gladly call at St Kilda, but if I cannot land you will have to stay on board till the end of the trip. It's up to you to take the chance; I will be sailing in an hour's time.' This was an opportunity I could not miss and I was only a day behind schedule. We set off round the Butt of Lewis, past the Flannan Isles and on to St Kilda. The wind rose during the night and we hove to at the back of Dun until eight a.m., when we sailed into the bay. The Captain blew the trawler's siren, but no one seemed to make an effort to come out to us. We could see the party on the island, but they did not realise why we were hooting the siren. Eventually, as we persisted blowing the ship's siren, we saw them launching a boat out. On board was His Lordship but he just looked at me and said nothing. He got into conversation with the Captain. Only my own native islanders spoke to me and asked how I missed the *Hebrides* the day before. They thought it was quite amusing. Only when we got ashore did His Lordship ask what had happened. I explained as best I could. 'Well, MacDonald, I really intended to sack you when I got home, but when I saw your face on the trawler I thought differently. I could see you had a rough passage and I am glad you are here now,' he said. 'I don't know how I would have fared without you.' So the incident was forgotten and I was reprieved.

We all had a wonderful time lobster fishing, shooting seals, catching and ringing puffins and roaming all over the hills of the island. Lord and Lady Dumfries's party consisted of the Marchioness of Bute, Miss Howie, the Hon. W. Stirling, Mr Drummond, Father MacMillan (a priest from Barra), a cook named Carruthers and myself. Also on the island were A.G. Ferguson, Finlay MacQueen, and Neil Gillies who helped look after the party. Unfortunately, after about a week's stay, our cook met with an accident and broke his collarbone while trying to shoot a seal out in the bay. He had not kept the gun tight enough to his shoulder when he pulled the trigger, with the result that it kicked back, whence the cause of his injury. He was sent back to the mainland for a doctor's attention on the first ship that called, and did not return. I was then left solely in charge, having to look after the whole party, to cook and clean the house where they stayed and to attend to their wants. I'm afraid there was not much variety in my kind of cooking, which was mostly tinned food, but there were plenty of 'spirits' which kept the party happy.

The priest slept in the schoolhouse on a camp bed. I had strict orders from His Lordship when we made up the priest's bed to slip a 'dram of whisky' under his pillow, as a night cap. The priest was a jolly old man, a very good religious Catholic man.

On Sunday we, the St Kildans, held a Gaelic service in our old church and the service was taken over by A.G. Ferguson who preached for an hour. Lord Dumfries and his party, being

Lord and Lady Dumfries's party on St Kilda (Calum MacDonald is front right) (John MacDonald)

The Factor's house (Alasdair MacEachen)

Catholics, held their service and Mass in the old Factor's house which stood halfway between the church and the village. As I look back on the event I wonder which party's service our Lord in Heaven listened to? Or is man such a hypocrite as to believe that it is only his religion God listens to? However, we all got on well together while on the island and when the time of our departure came we were reluctant to leave. Life was so blissful and peaceful compared to the hurly-burly of city and town life.

After three years in private service with His Lordship I decided to leave and find service in another private establishment; to get more experience, in the hope that one day I could become a butler. I applied to domestic agencies in Glasgow and was put in touch with Major Parson of Ford Bank, Johnstone, Paisley, and was employed by him as footman. It was a much smaller homestead than Dumfries House. They kept a smaller staff and did not entertain on the same scale as Lord Dumfries. I received a bigger weekly wage of £2 a week plus allowance for laundry, etc. The butler was a very experienced man and he taught me quite a lot. The Major had another country estate at Southend, Argyll. His

Lord and Lady Dumfries's holiday home on St Kilda, which they named Oiseval House, was previously the manse (Alasdair MacEachen)

wife was one of the family of 'Glencoats' of Paisley, a very famous name in Scotland. They had two sons and spent each summer at Southend where they had a small yacht, which we sometimes sailed up the Clyde and around the island of Arran. Myself and another employee on his estate were the only members of the crew. I thoroughly enjoyed those sailing trips.

Chapter 11

When the war broke out in 1939, Major Parson informed us we were to be dismissed as he would not be requiring our services and that he would only be keeping on the elderly butler, cook and maid.

I then returned to my home in Stornoway and started work with my brother as barman in my brother-in-law's pub. I did not like the life very much, so I left and got a job in the tweed mill, which I did not care for much either. There I met an Aberdonian married to a Stornoway girl and we became friends. He did not care for the work either. We applied to the Unemployment Exchange for a job in Invergordon where we were to start work tunnelling through the mountain. We reported at the office of the works and were engaged to start the following day. We were issued with blankets, etc. and shown the hut where we were to live. There were about ten dirty-looking navvies lying about the place, some snoring in their bunks. We sat silent on our bunks for a while, not saying a word, and nobody spoke to us. At last I said, 'Come on, let's make up our bunks and get some sleep.' My friend gave me one pathetic look and said, 'Mac, I would rather walk the moor all night than sleep in this hut.' He then looked around again and said, 'It would break my wife's heart if she knew I was sleeping among such dirt, let's get out of it.' 'Well,' I said, 'I am not too keen on the place, either.' We went back to the employment office on the site and demanded our employment cards. After an embarrassing argument with the clerk, he handed them over to us. We walked down the mountainside, carrying our cases towards town. My friend said, 'I'm going back to Stornoway, where are you making for?' I said, 'Glasgow.' When we arrived in town the last train for the day had left for Inverness, where we were to part company and go our separate ways.

We began to look for lodgings for the night and found it impossible as the town was overcrowded with army and naval personnel. We met a policeman and asked if we could spend the night in his jail. 'No,' he said, 'but if you want the address of a friend of mine, I will give it to you and just tell him I sent you.' He wrote the address down on a bit of paper and handed it to us. We thanked him and off we went in search of the address. A very charming lady opened the door. When we told her who sent us, she took us in and showed us our room. It was small but looked like a room in a castle compared to the navvy hut we were supposed to have slept in that night. The lady called us at seven a.m. to catch the morning train to Inverness, with a nice cup of tea, toast and beans, for which she only charged us fifteen shillings each; but we gave her a pound each, for a good night's sleep and a clean bed. We parted at Inverness and I carried on to Glasgow. I never met my friend again.

After a few days in Glasgow I was employed in the Rolls Royce factory in Hillington, as a trainee, making parts of aircraft engines. It was a fascinating experience, seeing a whole Rolls Royce engine being made and put together. It was a job I kept till the end of the war. While I was in the factory I received a letter from home which said that my brother John was seriously ill. I got permission from the manager to take my annual holidays and go home to Stornoway. He was unconscious when I arrived. The family doctor did not give him much chance of recovering, unless he was taken to Edinburgh Royal Infirmary, for brain surgery. The family decided to give him the chance. The doctor made all the necessary arrangements with the specialist in Edinburgh. His eldest son of sixteen and I agreed we would take him there. We left Stornoway that same night and got to Edinburgh the following evening at six p.m., where an ambulance was there to meet us. The next day his son returned home, but I took lodgings in the city to be at hand, in case I was needed. I visited him every day but he never regained consciousness at any time. Two days later the doctor told me there was nothing he could do for him, that he had a brain tumour and only a matter of days to live. The doctor was most sympathetic and kind and he told me he would arrange for my brother to be put in a home. I told the doctor I was sorry, but I could not let him be put in a home and I was going to take him back to his own home in Stornoway. It was a sad blow to all the family and to our hopes.

I immediately phoned my second eldest brother in Stornoway who asked me to try and get him home alive. He said to try and get an ambulance to take him to Kyle of Lochalsh where he would meet us and we would then take him on the mail boat *Lochness* to Stornoway. It was very difficult to find a private ambulance to travel so far across Scotland in war time. Then I thought if I went to see Lord Dumfries's old chauffeur at Charlotte Square, he might manage to find me an ambulance, for he knew the city and its garages better than I did. He was most helpful and told me not to worry, he would find me a private ambulance and off he went in search. He soon returned and told me he had found one who was willing to make the trip, but it would have to have two chauffeurs, as the journey was very long. The following morning we collected my brother and started our journey across Scotland to the west coast, following the road to Kyle.

After we passed Glencoe, we came to an Army post. Two soldiers stopped us and informed us that we could not proceed any further on that road as it was a Government Prohibited area and we needed a 'Pass' to get through. We explained our errand of mercy and that we had to catch the mail boat at Kyle by four p.m. We explained that the patient was an old soldier of the 1914 war and that he was unconscious and dying. They told us to wait while they got in touch with their headquarters by phone. When they came back they said it was no use, we would have to make a detour of twenty miles as they could not let us pass. Rather harsh treatment, I thought, for one of their own. The two chauffeurs were most sympathetic to me as I was concerned that the mail boat would not wait for us. By making the detour across the moorland road we were going to be late. Fortunately we made good time speeding along and when we arrived at Kyle the mail boat was waiting for us, half an hour on sailing. Once we got my brother on board, she moved off. I felt grateful to her Captain and the ambulance drivers for their humanitarian patience. My brother died two days later without regaining consciousness, and I later returned to the factory in Glasgow.

Shortly after one of the German raids on Glasgow, I visited my old uncle Finlay MacQueen and my auntie, Annie Ferguson, in Kincardine, Fife. As I walked up the garden path, he was sitting

Donald John Ferguson and Finlay MacQueen (Neil Ferguson)

in a chair in front of their house. His first greeting to me was, 'And how is your navel, son?' He then said, 'You won't be seeing your old Uncle much longer, I am getting old but you will always remember me when you undress and look at your tummy and don't you forget it.' 'No,' I said, 'but how are you?' He was getting old by this time; his great, black beard was now snowy white. 'Well,' he said, 'I sit here day after day, just thinking of the days long ago on our dear island. Today I have no one to speak to, except the family living in the house with me. People pass by and wave to me, but I cannot converse with them as I have only Gaelic, but I am old and will soon be at rest.' 'Oh,' I said, 'you must not be so morbid; you have many more years yet to come.' He was not really listening to me and said, 'These devils [meaning the German planes] passing over at night to bomb Glasgow worry me a lot. It's a sad world we are living in.' He then carried on: 'Do you see that hand?', putting out his right hand, 'that hand shook hands with the King of Great

Neil and Mary Ann Ferguson with their daughter Anne at Kincardine, Fife (Neil Ferguson)

Britain and if only I had the English tongue that day I would have told him, "My boy, you had better look out, the Germans are after you". I said, 'When did you shake hands with the King?' He said, 'At the Empire Exhibition in Glasgow, in 1938. I was introduced to him.' 'And how could you have told him?' I said, 'The war did not start until 1939.' 'Well,' he said, 'I dreamt it, but everyone I told of my dream would not believe me.' He was very, very proud that he, Finlay MacQueen from Hirta, shook hands with the King of Great Britain. He died a year after I visited him. On the day I visited them, there were five of my relations living in that house, but today they are all gone. The last, a Neil Ferguson, died on 28th June 1976, and he was the last Ferguson born on St Kilda before it was evacuated in 1930. There are several descendants of the Ferguson clan alive and scattered about Scotland.

Chapter 12

At the end of the war I was made redundant and returned home to Stornoway. After three months holiday, I saw an advertisement for a footman with a Miss Campbell in Ayr. I wrote for the situation and was taken on. While there I received a letter from Lord Dumfries's secretary, asking me if I cared to take over as butler-valet with His Lordship at Kames Castle, Rothesay, at a salary of £4 per week, which I duly accepted. When I arrived, I was much greeted by the family and made welcome. Lady Fiona was an addition to the family since I first left and was still at home. The boys, however, were now grown up and attending college. The staff were mostly strangers to me, but we soon got to know each other. Food was still rationed but we had our own home farm and garden which was a great asset to the French chef. The Lord and Lady did not entertain on the same lavish scale as before the war but the chef could still produce a very tasty dish for the dining room table. Instead of a footman to help me in the butler's pantry, one of the maids was my helper. Later on she became my wife, but it was not love at first sight; in fact it was quite the reverse, as she thought I was too strict in carrying out my duties. His Lordship decided he needed a footman and asked if I knew anyone for the job. I recommended my nephew who was discharged from the Army. He duly arrived and I taught him his duties as footman, which he soon picked up and carried out most efficiently.

Her Ladyship kept two nanny goats as pets, which roamed at will around the castle grounds. They were the most mischievous, playful animals I ever came across. If they found any door open,

Kames Castle, Isle of Bute (David Ross, www.britainexpress.com)

they would run about the passages and it was quite a job to get them to return outside. I usually set the dining room table for dinner in the afternoons. It was a long, highly polished oak table and after laying out the silverware, table mats, napkins, etc. one afternoon I finished the table by putting two vases of flowers on it and it looked extremely beautiful. I then went back to the butler's pantry, just off the dining room, to attend to other necessary jobs. Suddenly I heard a commotion in the dining room, looked in and there on top of my laid table were the two nanny goats and everything topsy turvy. The wine glasses smashed on the floor, the silverware and mats scattered everywhere, the vases on their sides and the two friends munching away at the fresh flowers. They gave me one look, jumped off the table with a 'Blaa, blaa,' and ran outside, jumping in the air. I saw red and I ran after them – why I don't know, as I could never catch them anyway. I imagined their 'Blaa, blaa' meant 'It's your own fault, you left the outside door open, so what do you expect of a goat.'

On another occasion they nearly scared the living daylights out of Jimmy, the chauffeur. In the courtyard of the castle was a tower, which had three floors. On the ground floor was the gunroom and gameroom and on the other two floors were bedrooms for the chauffeur and footman. As we had no footman at the time, the chauffeur slept in the tower on his own. To get to the rooms, there was a very narrow stone stairway and a rope hung down from the top which was used as a handrail. One night he was asleep, when he was suddenly awakened by a most unusual noise coming from up the stairs. His bedroom door was not quite closed and then all of a sudden the door opened wide. He sat up in the bed but could not see as the room was so dark. Into his bed jumped the two nanny goats. He thought it was the devil himself. When he heard the 'Blaa, blaa' he realised what it was, jumped out of the bed and chased them down the stairs. One can only imagine what a fright he must have got.

Her Ladyship also kept hens. One certain hen had a brood of young chicks, one of which was tiny and more delicate than the others. It had a bare, patched bottom, and everyone said it was diseased and should be killed. I felt pity for the poor thing and did not agree. I fed, nursed and watched over it and I talked to it every time I was near it. She seemed so forlorn beside the other chicks. Gradually it grew up, and became very tame. It followed me like a pet dog, even when I went for a walk in the castle grounds. If I was working in the pantry and the window was open, it would jump up on the window and perch there, clucking away, looking in on me all the time. It grew up to be a fully grown white hen. My bedroom was also on the ground level and it would jump up on that window too. Sometimes as I lay on the bed for a rest, it would sit there watching me, softly clucking away, as much as to say, 'What are you lying there for, instead of going for a walk?' One day we heard an awful sound of clucking coming from my bedroom. One of the maids, the chauffeur and myself went to investigate what the commotion was about. I opened the door to my bedroom and we could hardly believe our eyes. There on the bed was my hen, walking slowly around an egg she had laid in the middle of the bed. Every one of us let out a roar of laughter and the hen kept on clucking as hens do after laying an egg. She seemed to be saying, 'That's for you.' When His Lordship and Her Ladyship heard what had happened, they also laughed; it was a great joke all round. But I thought it was a wonderful reward from my pet hen.

As staff, we had to make our own fun. One winter night the chauffeur thought we would give two of the maids, who were off duty for the evening, a scare. We knew they would be returning from the pictures in Rothesay on the last bus at about ten-thirty p.m. The castle's drive was long and dark. We got a white bedroom sheet each and hid behind the trees which surrounded the place. We heard them approaching, then we jumped out, moaning and running from tree to tree. They stopped in their tracks, not sure if it was ghosts or not. In the end they realised who we were, but they agreed that we had given them a scare at first.

My dear mother died in 1946, soon after I rejoined Lord Dumfries, and I went home to the funeral. This, then, was my last tie with a promise I made to myself, that I would never marry while she was alive. I was thirty-eight years of age now and still a bachelor. I became more friendly with the Irish maid, named Marie Doyle, who used to help me in the pantry and who certainly did not like me in those days. Yet we had a lot in common, as our backgrounds were very similar in many ways. Her parents came from a country background in Eire. We both liked the outdoor life and often went cycling round the Isle of Bute. Our temperaments sometimes clashed, but never seriously, and of course it was natural, with her being Irish and me a Scot.

She was a good few years younger than me and gradually our friendship developed to the courting stage – whereby man and woman by instinct learn they are meant for each other, and always want to be in each other's company. At no time did we talk of marriage, but we did decide to leave Scotland and go to London.

In the paper I saw an advert for a valet with an Italian film producer in Taplow, Bucks. I applied for an interview by letter and received, by return post, the interview offer. I did not inform His

Lordship, but I did tell his private secretary of my intentions and stated I would give a month's notice in the event of my acceptance of the situation. This was my first ever trip to London and I had some difficulty in making my way from Euston to Taplow, but I made it. A chauffeur driven car was supposed to meet me at Taplow station. When I arrived, there was no car in sight, but I met a gentleman who directed me to the right road. As I walked along the country road, a car drew up slowly beside me and the driver asked me if I was MacDonald. I said, 'Yes,' and he told me to get inside and that he had missed me at the station and was sorry. We arrived at the house soon after and I was introduced to the butler. He ordered me some food and refreshment and afterwards escorted me into the gentleman's study. His study was set like a stage. He looked down on me from behind his desk and wore a pair of glasses resting on the end of his nose, a beautiful dressing gown and a cigarette in a cigarette holder in his mouth. He welcomed me and hoped I had a good journey. After surveying me for a while he said, 'Yes, MacDonald, I think you will be suitable for my valet. I travel a good deal, often to America, and you would have to travel with me. Now, tell me, what wages are you getting at your present job, and why are you leaving His Lordship?'

I explained that my wages were £4 a week. Without any hesitation, he barked out, 'I shall give you the same wages.' I was rather taken aback, as I expected at least a more generous offer. I explained, 'Sir, I will have to think it over and I will let you know whichever way I decide. I have to give a month's notice to my present employer.' He agreed and I was dismissed. It did not take me long to decide, once I was out of his presence. I thought he was a pompous 'ass,' and rather mean with it.

I returned to Rothesay that same night by train and duly arrived back at Kames Castle on the following afternoon. The same evening Her Ladyship sent for me in the dining room and began giving me a dressing down. She accused me of having played 'a very dirty trick' on His Lordship. I asked her to explain what she meant. She said, 'You went to London for an interview without letting His

Lordship know, and I think it was a very dirty thing to do.' 'Yes,' I said, 'but I told his secretary I was going for an interview and if it was a suitable situation I would give His Lordship a month's notice, therefore I did not think it necessary to say more till I had the interview.' In the circumstance I did not like to be accused of playing a dirty trick, as I have never played a dirty trick on anyone in my life. She was very mad with me and dismissed me very coldly. I knew it was time to look ahead for the atmosphere would never be the same again. Later on I learned that the gentleman from Taplow had phoned His Lordship while I was still travelling back from my interview to enquire as to my character, in which case my opinion of the man in the first place was well founded.

My wife-to-be gave in her notice of leave and left for London in May. The understanding between us was that if she found a suitable job, I would follow and we would get married. She phoned me regularly and one day she said she had good news for me. If I gave His Lordship a month's notice and came to London, we could get married, as she had found a nice situation from an agency. A Mr and Mrs Phillip Goldburg of 4 The Manor, Davis Street, needed a married couple to look after their flat; also we would have a bedsitter of our own. This was the kind of opportunity we were seeking so without further delay, I handed in to His Lordship my month's notice of resignation. By now he had become the Marquis of Bute on the death of his father the year before. He rang for me to come and see him in the dining room and enquired as to why I wanted to resign. I explained my reasons and he accepted gracefully. He wished us happiness and prosperity and added, 'MacDonald, I have come to like you a lot and I regret you are leaving me. If I had a cottage to offer you both, would you consider staying with me?' I replied, 'Thank you, my Lord, but it's our wish to start a new life for ourselves, and London seems a good place to start. My nephew William, the footman, is a good chap and he will look after you as I tried.' And so he did; he was promoted to butler as soon as I left and he served His Lordship for eight more years.

Chapter 13

At the end of my month's notice, I left Kames Castle and came down to London. We got married on 5th July 1947, at St Dunstan's Catholic Church, Chiswick. It was a very quiet affair, for neither of us knew many friends in London. Our honeymoon was taken up with exploring London and visiting the museums and parks. On 15th July we started our married life, working for the Goldburgs. They were charming employers, who had two daughters and who did not entertain a lot, so we had plenty of leisure hours to see the sights. The following summer we went to Ireland; it was my first visit to the 'Emerald Isle' and I fell in love with it and with my in-laws. My wife's home was in Bray, Co. Wicklow, close to the coast. The first day we climbed Brayhead, up to the cross which stands on the top, where you can see for miles around. The view is wonderful from up there; you can see as far away as Howth, Dublin and the Sugar Loaf Mountains in the opposite direction and the beautiful, green valleys thereabouts. Sitting on top of Brayhead reminded me so much of my native isle, St Kilda, that I felt I just wanted to live there always. We have been over on holiday there every other year since and have travelled most of the country since then. We have never travelled abroad; it's been one year Ireland and the other year Scotland.

In 1949 we had to look for another situation as my wife had become pregnant and No. 4 The Manor was not suitable for a child. I went to the Mayfair Agency to see if they had a vacancy suitable for a couple with a child. After a couple of days I was invited to call at the office for an interview with a lady and gentleman who wanted a butler. There was also a free cottage as part of any agreement settled. This was excellent news and we both felt really happy at the prospect of a cottage of our own. Two days afterwards I kept the appointment in the agency office and was introduced to a Mr and Mrs Coriat, who had a house called Twattley in Malmesbury. I took a dislike to the gentleman once I was introduced. His first question was, 'Were you in the Army?' I said, 'No, Sir.' His second question was, 'And why were you not?' 'Well, Sir,' I said, 'I was working in a factory making engines, which

The marriage of Malcolm (Calum) MacDonald and Marie Doyle at St Dunstan's, Chiswick, London on 5th July 1947
(Neil Ferguson)

was just as essential to the war effort as fighting in the Army.' The lady said to her husband, 'There is no need for such questions, I think he will suit us fine, as he has the experience we require.' Then she turned to me and asked, 'When could you start work for us?' 'I must give a fortnight's notice, will that suit you?' 'Yes, that will do fine, and we will expect you then in a fortnight's time. You will have a furnished cottage which is centrally heated and a garden close to the stables, but quite near the house. I think you will like it.' My wife asked me when I returned from the interview how I got on. I said, 'It looks very promising and I like the lady, but I cannot say too much for the gentleman, he seems to have too much self-importance. But we shall give it a try and see how things work out. My wages will be £6 a week plus the free cottage.'

We arrived at Malmesbury, and took a taxi to Twattley and our cottage. Everything seemed nice and homely and we thought we were very lucky and got settled in. We reported that we had arrived and were shown around the place. I met the rest of the staff which consisted of the valet, oddman, pantrymaid, housekeeper, maid and a chef who came from Aberdeen, as well as a nanny and a lady's-maid. After I had spoken to the chef in the kitchen, he informed me he was leaving in a week's time. I asked him what it was like to work for my employers and his reply amazed me. He said, 'You will soon find out.' He also said, 'I will give you a month here and no longer, in that time you will find out for yourself.' I thought he was kidding me on, but I soon did find out he told me the truth. When I arrived back at the cottage my wife asked me, 'Well – what do you think of the staff and the place?' I said, 'From what I gather especially from the chef, I have a feeling our personalities will clash one day and we will not be staying long. But today everyone was very nice to me and I do like the run of the place. I gather that Mrs Coriat was married before and was known as Lady Penelope Curnow. Also that Mr Coriat was only a land agent. They have three girls of school age, the two eldest from her first marriage and the third from this marriage. I have a part-time parlour-maid to give me a hand in the pantry and they do not entertain much, only the occasional house-party when he goes fox-hunting.'

We came to know the elderly groom and his wife, as they lived close by. Mr Coriat had an estate office in part of the same surroundings as us and he spent most of his time between the office and his study in the house. He looked the real country squire in his tweed jacket and breeches and he carried a cane. When he went out walking he had two dogs following behind at his heels. One day he phoned me from his office and said, 'I want all my staff out on the lawn at eleven a.m.' I had no idea what it was all about so we all gathered: head groom, gardener, labourer, the oddman and everyone else. We all stood to attention in a row like a lot of soldiers. He came along like an Army General. He addressed us as follows: 'Someone has taken my motor van from the garage without my permission and I want that person to step forward and explain why he did it.' We all looked at each other in amazement at such ridiculous behaviour from a gentleman to his staff, each of us denying any knowledge of the charge. He dismissed us with the authoritative remark, 'I shall find out and the person shall be dealt with.' That was the last we heard on the matter. Sometime later we heard it was his own nephew who took the van to town to do some messages.

As my wife was nearing confinement time, her mother came to be near at hand. She came from Ireland to stay with us. Mrs Coriat asked me as each day passed how my wife was and when the baby was due. I would thank her for her kindness and concern for my wife's welfare. When she was taken into the Malmesbury General Hospital four days before her confinement, I told Mrs Coriat. She asked me what I wanted, a boy or a girl. I told her I was happy whichever it was, it made no difference to us. On 7th May my son was born. My wife and I were so happy and so was my wife's mother as she was now a granny for the first time. The next day I told Mrs Coriat that we had a son and that they were both doing fine. 'Oh,' she said, 'You have a son and how lucky you are,' and she walked away. From that day on she never asked again after my wife and baby. I began to think how odd it was that she never asked after them and her attitude seemed to be cool and unfriendly towards me. I carried on with my duties as if nothing was amiss. Yet I felt annoyed and the atmosphere was depressing. I asked the nanny if she knew what it was all about. She answered, 'Don't you know? She is jealous, because you have a son and she has not, as she has always wanted a son.' I could hardly believe it was true.

A few days later, the phone rang while I was cleaning the silverware in the pantry. I picked up the receiver and a voice I did not recognise said, 'MacDonald?' I was still trying to think who it was so I answered slowly, 'Yes,' and loud and clear came the reply, 'Yes, Sir, when you speak to me!' I said, 'I'm sorry, Sir, I was trying to think whose voice it was.' 'Never mind whose voice it is, when you answer the phone you say "Yes, Sir".' 'Very good,' I said, 'What can I do for you, Sir?' 'Go to my desk in the study and you will find my diary on it, and I want you to give me a telephone number from it. I shall hold on till you come back.' This I did and passed on the information he wanted. I felt myself fuming with anger that I should be spoken to in such a rude manner for no real reason. Never in my years in private service had I been spoken to in such a way. I made up my mind that he was not going to get away with it. He had to walk past my pantry window to get to his study and I kept a watch out for him. He came along, the real country squire swinging his cane and the two dogs following behind. I waited till I thought he would be in his study and settled down at his desk. I put on my jacket and walked to his study and knocked. He called, 'Come in. What is it, MacDonald?' I replied, 'Sir, when you phoned earlier on, I did not know it was you on the line as I thought it was someone else. But for you, who is supposed to be a gentleman, to talk to me in such a rude manner, as if I was a slave; I tell you here and now, never again, Sir, address me in such a tone of voice.' He stood up behind his desk, flaming with anger. 'I will speak to you any way I feel like it and I have a good mind to slap your face.' 'Very well, Sir,' I said, 'since I hold out my face to you, go ahead and slap it. But it will be the last face you will ever slap. I have worked for real gentlemen, long before I came here to work for you. But I cannot say you are one.' I went on: 'You may be my employer but I am not your slave. You can sack me and that is all you can do.' He then calmed down and sat down. 'Well, MacDonald, we have both lost our tempers, shall we forget it?' 'Yes, Sir, I shall forget it, but Sir, what I said still goes. Never speak to me like a slave. I have also heard you speak so to some of your other staff and I cannot say I like it.' 'Alright, MacDonald, you may carry on as if nothing has happened.' 'Thank you, Sir,' I said, and walked out of his study.

For a few days things went smoothly, until one morning the postman was late. It was part of my duties to take the mail and his morning cup of tea sharp at seven a.m. to his sitting room upstairs. This particular morning the postman was about five minutes late in arriving, and as I was taking up the tea he arrived and handed me the letters, including the staff letters. I sorted them out, put the gentleman's on the tray and climbed the stairs. Halfway up I heard his voice, dark and loud: 'MacDonald, when I want my tea at seven o'clock I mean seven o'clock, not three minutes before or after but on the dot.' 'Sorry, Sir,' I said, 'the postman was a few minutes late this morning; that is why I am a few minutes late with your tea.' He said, 'That does not matter, when I say seven o'clock, I mean seven o'clock.' By now my temper also was up, and I laid the tray on the floor where he was standing in his silk dressing gown, looking down on me, and said, 'Sir, in future, if you wish to get your mail and tea on the stroke of seven and you do not allow me a couple of minutes either way to sort the mail out, you can just walk down the stairs and get your own tea. You are the most unreasonable person I have ever come across.' I walked down the stairs to the pantry. He must have been dumbfounded for he was muttering at the top of the stairs as I walked away and left him for I felt I had had enough of the place and wished I had never accepted the post of butler.

My wife was rather upset at the way things were going and so was her mother. We decided I would have to leave as the job as butler was becoming intolerable. We then decided it would be best for my wife and our son to go to Ireland with her mother until I could find some kind of work in London.

The confrontation between the Coriats and myself came a fortnight after our son was born. We had arranged he would be christened on the Sunday, by a Catholic priest, and we were going to have a small party for this very special important occasion in every family life. I arranged with my parlour-maid that she would stay and attend to Mr and Mrs Coriat from after lunch and set their tea in the afternoon and I would be back to serve them dinner that evening. She very kindly agreed to attend to their requirements.

We had our son christened John Patrick David, and afterwards we held our party in the cottage. The priest, my mother-in-law, the groom, his wife and the housekeeper came to the party and a nice, jolly one it was too. In the evening I went back to serve dinner to the Coriats and family at eight p.m. The parlour-maid informed me that they had gone to the hotel in Malmesbury to have dinner so I went back to our cottage, where everyone was still enjoying themselves, except the priest who had already left.

I started back to work on the Monday morning at six-thirty a.m. as usual, brought up the gentleman's morning tray at seven a.m. and set the dining room for breakfast. After breakfast was over and I was clearing away, Mrs Coriat came into the pantry to arrange some fresh flowers. As she kept arranging the flowers in different vases, she said, 'MacDonald?' I said, 'Yes, Ma'am?' 'Why did you tell Mrs Jones to stay on duty on Sunday while you went off?' she enquired. I was rather taken aback and replied, 'My Lady, yesterday was a special day for me and my wife, as we had our son christened.' 'Well,' she said, 'you should have asked me first before you made arrangements with Mrs Jones to stay on.' I said, 'Listen, My Lady, why should I tell you anything that concerns my family? Ever since the day of my wife's confinement when my son was born neither you nor Mr Coriat has once asked how they were getting on; and I as the Butler can arrange the staff under me to do any job that is necessary as long as your requirements are met. I only had four hours off and came back to serve the dinner and yet you did not inform me after lunch that you would be out to dinner. My Lady, I was told when I came here to work for you that I would not stay long. In fact this is the unhappiest place I have ever worked in and as from this moment I am no longer your employee.' She ran out of the pantry crying. I felt sorry for her, for I think she was a very unhappy woman and I liked her in a certain way, but I had had enough bigotry since I joined their service. I walked out and left.

When I told my wife and mother-in-law what had happened, the question was, 'What are we going to do?' The phone in the cottage rang; it was Mr Coriat who said, 'I want you out of there by mid-day tomorrow.' I replied, 'It will give me much pleasure,' and replaced the receiver. Next morning we all travelled back to London, to my sister who lived near the Oval. That evening my wife, son and mother-in-law went to Ireland while I stayed behind to look for a job in the city. After a few days, I got a temporary situation as houseman with a Mrs Mills, of South Street, off Park Lane. Her husband owned the 'Les Ambassadors' Club near Hyde Park Corner. She had met with an accident while skiing in Switzerland and sprained her ankle, and needed a temporary man in the house while she recuperated, for she entertained guests of the club while confined to the house. During the fortnight I was with her she entertained the film stars Tyrone Power and his wife, who were newly married; also Michael Wilding and Stewart Grainger. They were all friends of the Mills and were regularly at their club. Cooked meals were sent in from the club and I had to act as waiter and butler to these famous stars of the day.

I found Mrs Mills a very friendly individual, but at the end of the fortnight she was well enough to dispense with my services. She asked, could she do anything for me? I said no, I would look round on my own for something different from private service. It was not easy, so I signed on at the Labour Exchange at Brixton. After a week they advised me, with my kind of experience, to try the hotels and gave me a list of hotels to go to for an interview. Of the many I tried only Grosvenor House had a vacancy for a relief. I was taken to the manager's office, where I was asked about my past employment and if I had a reference I could show. I produced the only one I had. It was from Lord Bute, and it read as follows:

> Mount Stuart, Rothesay, Isle of Bute,
> 9th November 1948.
>
> To whom it may concern,
>
> Malcolm MacDonald was for several years in my employ as valet, footman and loader, and for a considerable period was in sole charge of plate and silver. In all the time he was with me he carried out his duties most efficiently. He is clean, sober and honest in every way, and I can personally vouch for his absolute integrity of character.
>
> He has travelled with me a good deal, and from experience I can say that he packs extraordinarily well, and looks after everything on the journey in such a way that his employer has nothing at all to worry about. Never have I known anything to go wrong either by land, sea or air, when MacDonald was with me.
>
> He is extraordinarily good with children and was a great favourite with my sons and daughter.
>
> He looked after my shooting dogs on many occasions, and did so extremely efficiently. In fact, animals appeared to take a ready liking to him. He left much to my regret when he got married, because at that time I had not a single vacant house on my estate to offer him.
>
> Should any further information be required I shall be pleased to furnish it.
>
> Signed: Bute.

Calum's work with animals included assisting in the relocation of over 100 sheep from Soay to the main island for the Marquis of Bute in 1932
(Alasdair MacEachen)

When the manager read it, he was much impressed and said, 'Have you got one from your last employer, Mr Coriat?' I said, 'No, and there is not any use asking for one.' To which he replied, 'Why? Have you been in prison?' His secretary, sitting at her desk, replied, 'No, it's nothing to do with anyone, it was a personal dispute. He has told me about Mr Coriat, and I don't think he would give him a reference either. And anyway, that reference from Lord Bute is good enough.' He then offered me the job as valet, which I accepted, and followed up with the question, 'What wages do you expect starting in the Hotel?' I said, 'I don't know, about seven or eight pounds a week?' 'Tut, tut,' he said, 'you will be earning far more than that.' This was great news to me and I was exceedingly excited at the prospect of informing my wife in Ireland that at last I had found a very good job, and that they would be able to return very soon to London. I was told to go and see the head valet, a Mr Smith, and if he was satisfied with me I could start the following Monday, which I did.

My first wages were around £14, plus tips, which brought it up to about £17. A week's wage was made up in three ways. The basic wage was £3.15.0*d*, then you received a quarter of your weekly pressings, plus commission, then plus tips. So the higher wage depended largely on how much you pressed each week, and the generosity of the guests with regard to tipping. Nowadays, of course, wages are much higher and a valet can earn up to £60 a week and sometimes £70 with overtime, but it was only since I retired that this happened. Still, I was very satisfied when I first started and I liked the job and meeting all kinds of people. I was able to give each guest whatever kind of service they requested; and one only worked eight hour shifts instead of all day long as in private service. Staff were provided with a uniform and their meals while on duty.

Now I was able to write to my wife and son in Ireland and tell them of my good fortune, and to return whenever they wished. A few days later she wrote back, saying how pleased and happy she was to hear of my success and hoped I was finished with private service for good, and that she would be back in London in a week's time.

We stayed with my sister at the Oval while we looked round for a home of our own. In a local paper we saw an advert, 'A flat in an old Victorian house on Wandsworth Road, with a large garden at back; present occupier going to Australia.' We went to see the place; it was very old looking from the outside, but it had a large bedroom, sitting room and kitchen, but no running water inside. The toilet and water for our use was in a shed outside. It was partly furnished and badly needed decorating. The lady wanted £100 for the key and furnishings and seventeen shillings weekly rent, to be paid to her old father who was living in the basement flat below. We considered the advantages: a place of our own and a garden for the family. We accepted her offer and handed over our little nest egg of £100 we had struggled to save. It was a good investment in the end, for when the council knocked down the old building years afterwards, we got a council flat across the road.

The family came along in the old house; besides John, Charles, Elizabeth and Marion were born there. In 1955 my wife's parents came over from Ireland for a month's holiday and we got rather crowded, but as the rooms were large and only John was of school age, we managed fairly well.

John started school at the end of summer, September 1955, at St Anne's Catholic School, Vauxhall. It was about three quarters of a mile walk from where we lived. His mother walked him to school each morning and took Charles with her for the walk, but left Elizabeth and Marion with her mother and father and myself to look after them till she came home.

The first morning turned out to be a morning she will never forget. She arrived at the school with all the other mothers and

The family group: Malcolm (Calum), mother-in-law, daughter Marion, wife Marie, daughter Elizabeth and sons John and Charles (the younger sons, Neil and Andrew, came along later) (Neil Ferguson)

they waited around until all the children went into school class. She had Charles by her side, as he was only four years old. After the children went into the school, she looked down to take Charles by the hand to walk home, but there was no sign of him anywhere to be seen. She asked the other mothers, but they had not seen him either. Thinking he may have gone into the class with his brother, she asked the teacher if he was there, but no, he seemed to have disappeared. By now she was getting panicky; she searched every corner of the school yard, in the church adjoining the school and in every classroom, to no avail. By this time she was frantic with anxiety and was more than sure that someone had abducted him. She then phoned Kennington Police Station in case someone had found him and reported it to the police. They had not received any message either. She came home crying and weeping; all she would say was, 'I lost Charles.' When she finally quietened down, she told what had happened. We were all stunned. I just could not believe such a thing could happen. I was sure he must be somewhere in the school. We all walked different ways back to the school and searched every corner and classroom again but there was not a sign of him. The traffic round Vauxhall is very busy at most times therefore we discarded the idea he was run over for we would have heard of any such accident. As we all stood on the street wondering where he could have got to, I said, 'Come, we will ring the police station again.' We went into a phone kiosk and phoned Kennington Police Station again. This time we were told to go to Union Row Police Station; that a panda car had picked up a child walking all on his own at Vauxhall. His description fitted Charles. We all jumped into a taxi which took us to Union Row, which was not far from where we lived. When we told the sergeant at the desk our story, he said, 'A boy of that age was picked up, he is in the yard playing with the horses and a policeman is with him.' He told us to go and have a look. Sure enough, there was our son, quite unconcerned about all the worry he had caused by straying away. It was quite a reunion with his mother and all of us.

Chapter 13

When all the children were attending school and able to go and come home on their own my wife suggested she would take a part-time job to help rear the children and also pass the time. We were now living in a new council flat. She took on part-time domestic work for various people in the city. It was a great asset to the family budget and holidays each year. She then took on a steady job as a maid at a block of flats at 40 Queen's Gate, from ten a.m. until four p.m. After a year she was asked to run the place as manageress. She asked for my advice as she was afraid she wasn't experienced enough to tackle such a responsibility. I told her to go ahead, that she had the brains and common sense to give it a try, which she did, and I am proud to say she never looked back. She developed a wonderful personality and has a brilliant alert mind and a photographic memory, which amazes me at times, and not only me, but her employers too. Even though the property has changed hands on three different occasions she has been maintained as manageress by each employer.

The place has prospered from the day she took over, and most of her guests are very rich Arabs from the Middle East. She is known as Mrs Mac to them all, including the Arabian Embassy in London. Many other guests from all over the world come to stay at Queen's Gate and once they have come in contact with Mrs Mac, they always return to her. Two very rich Arabs invited themselves to dinner with us at our home in Wandsworth Road. It was great fun trying to carry on a conversation with them as they only spoke a little English and we spoke no Arabic at all. My wife has risen to great heights, from a fifteen-shillings-a-week-wage maid at Kames Castle, to today with her own staff of maids working for her. They get better treatment than she did when she was a maid. Her outlook on life has not changed through the years; she gives the same treatment to rich and poor alike, whatever their creed or colour. Some of her guests include very prominent people from the Middle East, America and throughout the world. Each of her guests receives the same courtesy and attention, and her Irish sense of humour outrides any diplomacy expected to be given; a prince or rich sheik, they all receive the same treatment.

Chapter 14

In 1967, I made my last trip to St Kilda and took my eldest son, John, with me. We joined a party from the National Trust for Scotland. It was my son's first visit to his ancestral island and it meant great excitement to look forward to. The party was in great spirits when we met in Mallaig where we all joined the boat that would take us there. It was not the most comfortable boat in which to make such a journey. We all sat on deck till we reached Lochmaddy, where we stayed for the night. In the early morning we left Lochmaddy and we all came on deck, where we sat for the next eight hours till we reached St Kilda. It was cold and uncomfortable, with sea mist most of the way. Once we went through the Sound of Harris and headed into the Atlantic we drifted a bit off course with the running tide instead of a straight course which would have brought us in between Levenish and Boreray and the Stacs of Armin and Lee, to get our bearings. We could not see much ahead for a while as the mist was all around us, but we knew we were in the vicinity of the islands, for we could smell the guano of the gannets and the other birds which nest there. Gradually we could see all the islands. We started our engines again and sailed close to Boreray. How familiar they all were to me, and how happy I was, as I tried to explain to my son the different islets and rocks as we passed by and on towards the main island and bay. It was two p.m. when we came to a stop in the bay and, to everyone's relief, the boat finally stopped rolling from side to side in the waves.

The Army rubber boats came out to meet us and take us ashore, but we all had to put a life belt on before we left our own boat. As we landed on the quay, the Army Captain greeted us and wished us a happy fortnight. On learning I was born on St Kilda he came over and asked me how it felt to be back home. I told him I was very, very happy to visit the place once more, but was rather sad at not seeing any of the old familiar faces to greet me and that otherwise the place looked the same, apart from the Army huts near the shore and strange faces all around me.

We all in turn did the cooking each day, mostly out of cans. The mornings were taken up by repairing and tarring the roofs of the houses, which had been re-roofed by previous parties. The rest of the day you were free to roam about the island.

It was a nostalgic visit for me, even though the party was very cheerful and my son was with me. As I walked on my own one day through the village street, stepping into every ruined house, I had vivid memories of each and every family who had occupied each house in my youth and recalled their greetings, and now only ghosts remained. As I walked into the cemetery where rested my

The entrance to the cemetery on St Kilda (Alasdair MacEachen)

two sisters and my forefathers, it was a sad experience, which I tried to hide from the rest of the party.

When we went climbing the hills, I discovered I was no longer the energetic youth I once was. I was always lagging and trailing behind, out of breath for want of exercise. But then again, I was much older than any of the others in the party and the pace they put up was too much for me, so perhaps I have to be excused.

As we sat at lunch one day someone suggested we should try a cooked fulmar or puffin as a change of diet and that I should cook it as we did when I lived there and dined on them as a youth. The member of the party who suggested it thought I would love to taste the old delicacy which was my staple food as a youth and that of my forefathers before me. The leader of the party said we were not allowed to kill the birds. Though I did not reply, I felt it was an insult to me to be told I could not eat the food I had been brought up on and generations of my fellow islanders before me, because the National Trust said so. I asked the question, 'Are the birds of the air more important than human beings? Did the National Trust object to the killing of these same birds when we lived on the island?' No, they did not care less how many birds we killed and ate for food, so why the concern now, for these same birds? Again I asked the question, 'Do they object to the killing and shooting of grouse, snipe and pheasants by the rich on Scottish moors every year? Or is there a law for the rich and another for the poor?' I often wonder. I do not blame our leader on the island for saying we could not have a dinner of fulmar or puffin as it was an order given to him. In my case, as a native of the island, I felt I had every right to have a meal of my favourite dish with or without having to ask permission from anyone. If anyone had dared to say, when we islanders lived on the island as families, that you must not kill the birds, he would have been lashed and sent scurrying back to whence he came. That was how I felt sitting at the table, but I kept my place for the sake of any embarrassment to all concerned.

The Army added to our excitement by taking us up to Mullach Sgar by jeep to wait for a plane coming in from Benbecula, which dropped the mail from about 100 feet up; it circled overhead and flew back to Benbecula after the drop. The Army Captain kept up a conversation with the pilot by radio all the time. For such a thing to have happened in my forefathers' day would have been a miracle, and if they had been told it would happen one day, they would have called you a 'crank'. On another occasion they entertained us at the station by first giving us a drink at their special bar and then by showing us a film; an evening well spent. I even had the pleasure of phoning London and spent a few minutes talking to my family, who were so surprised and excited that they could hardly believe it was from Hirta I was speaking to them. On Sunday the Army Chaplain held a service in the old familiar church. The preacher's pulpit is still there, also the smaller box pulpit which my father used as a Precentor, to lead the singing in Gaelic, but there are only a few of the congregation's pews to be seen. Where they disappeared to, I did not find out. It was a pity they were removed, as it gave the church an empty look. Yet as I looked around the once holy place, I could imagine and see and hear the ghosts of the past vividly. When the service was over we were all invited to the Army Mess for some refreshments and a chat. The trip was wonderful and exciting for my son; he enjoyed every day of it. It was all too brief, but it gave him an inward sight of my kind of life as a boy compared to his in the city of London. Here nature led you by the hand through the four seasons of the year, one was born free and Mother Nature took charge of you.

On returning to London, my son John took part in the Duke of Edinburgh's Gold Award by climbing Mount Snowdon in Wales. He was presented with the medal at Buckingham Palace, a very proud moment for him and us.

He joined the Police Cadets at Hendon, where he passed out as a Police Officer, and he is now attached to Willesden Police Station. He played rugby for the Metropolitan Police for a couple of years and he also plays for the London Scottish and toured the USA in 1976 with them and won a silver cup. In 1971 he married a Miss Haley Waterworth, who represented London in the Rose of Tralee competition in the same year. They have a son named Stuart, who was born in 1973 and looks as if he is going to be another born rugby player for the future. He is five years younger than my youngest son, born in 1968.

In 1973 my second eldest son, Charles, married Miss Susanne Gouldsmith, a policeman's daughter. He is now a qualified chartered accountant and they live in Australia, after emigrating in 1976.

My eldest daughter, Elizabeth, is a hairdresser, and Marion is a staff nurse at Westminster Hospital. Neil is an apprentice plasterer, and Andrew is still at school.

Chapter 15

At this stage in my life I feel I have a lot to be thankful for, as I look back over the years since I first started out on life's journey, until my retirement in 1976. Most of the credit is due to my cool-headed wife and her devotion as a wife and mother in rearing a happy family and who, without scholarship, through her own initiative, has achieved great success in life.

Neither of us belonged to a trade union or any other organisation and I begin to wonder how it is that people like us can go through life and live in a city like London, where there is such a 'hullaballoo' in all walks of life and where we are surrounded by trade unionists. I may be wrong but it's my conviction that if a man is prepared to face life and give his best in any kind of work and not to depend on unions and the rule of the book, he could achieve far more benefit from life and independence than just sticking to rules and relying on others.

Working in a hotel brings one into contact with many kinds of fellow beings of all creeds and colours. Some stand high on their own special pedestals, but when you speak to them and look at them, you realise they are all mortals like everyone else. In my lowly capacity as a valet I have met very famous names: America's Cardinal Spellman, Rev. Billy Graham the evangelist, Margaret Lockwood, Doris Day, Shirley MacLaine, Ray Milland, Rock Hudson, Tony Curtis, Peter Falk, His Highness the Sultan of Brunei and family, His Highness Sultan of Johore and family, George Formby, Captain Townsend, Sir Oswald Mosley, Jackie Stewart and many more. All were very charming, sincere people.

I have also met some others who were the opposite of charming or sincere, who were staying for the sake of having a good time with their women friends for the night; like the hairy ape of a Dane who offered me the woman he slept with all night and in the morning she lay stretched out on a couch in her birthday suit. I walked away, wondering what kind of a brute he was, who would say such a thing.

Others were selfish and mean and could not care less for other guests; as long as they got full attention, the rest could wait. But there were the exceptions whom I felt were real personal friends, like the late Sir Gerald Nabarro MP, Comm. E. H. Walker, Mr Faggort and others who would chat with one in the most friendly way. These were guests who came regularly and were a pleasure to look after.

Through the twenty-six years of my employment with Grosvenor House, I have seen many changes in all sections and departments since it went to central service. Gone are the days when one gave special service to the guests on his own floor, many of whom were regulars, and when the waiters were dressed in black swallow tails, stiff collars, cuffs and black bow ties and served with grace their floor guests year in, year out. Today the waiters dress in short green jackets, bluish trousers and soft shirts with ordinary collars. Most are of foreign origin and their attitude is far less graceful than the old days. As one guest, whom I have known nearly as long as I worked there, said, 'Mac, what has happened to Grosvenor House? No one seems to care anymore. Your table is set down in your room with the attitude of "Take it or leave it" and the waiter walks away.' 'Yes,' I said, 'I agree with you, that is the attitude nowadays. As you notice, it's mostly foreign service now, gone is the courtesy one gave when you stayed here long ago; the outlook on life has changed also.'

As she walked away she remarked, 'I am glad you are still here, but, Mac, I don't think we will be coming much longer, as it has lost that homely feeling.' In a sense that was true, but it is still one of the most popular hotels in London. Take for example the two guests I heard talking to each other as they stood waiting for the lift to take them down to the lobby. One asked the other, 'Where are you staying?' The other fellow replied, 'At the Hilton, but it is not the same as the Grosvenor House, the atmosphere here is more homely.' I formed the conclusion from their conversation that, even with all the changes that had taken place, some guests still find it a happy place to stay in London.

Through life one meets many a fellow man and finds it very difficult to assess his character, wealth or his way of living; or if he is genuine or a fraud. Two incidences I came across are worth mentioning:

The first happened one evening when I first came to live in the old house in Wandsworth Road. My wife was out and I was looking after the family. Around ten p.m. a knock sounded at the door. I opened it and there stood a vagrant or beggar; a well-built man. I asked him what he wanted. He said, 'Can you give me a few shillings for the night?' I replied, 'No, I am afraid I can't, I have a young family to keep, but are you hungry?' 'Yes,' he said. 'When did you last eat?' I asked. 'Not since early morning,' he grumbled. Then I said, 'Come in and I will cook you something.'

He followed me into the kitchen and sat down. Judging by his appearance he looked well fed to me. However, I proceeded to fry him a couple of bacon rashers and eggs with toast and butter. I made a pot of tea and set it on the table in front of him. I tried to converse with him, but he kept moaning and grumbling and feeling sorry for himself. He would not tell me anything about himself so I left him alone, wondering if I was wise to let him come in. Later I said, 'I shall make some sandwiches to take with you?' and proceeded to do so, half a loaf with cheese, which I put in a paper bag. When he finished, I offered him a cigarette, which he took. As he was leaving I gave him the sandwiches and two shillings, he grunted a kind of thanks and walked out into the night. When my wife came home, I told her of my guest for supper. She remarked, 'You must be mad letting anyone of that kind into the house; I cannot even trust you to look after the house when I am away.' Next morning as I went out to work, there in the front garden, scattered about the bushes, were the sandwiches and cheese I had given to my guest the night before. Never again, I thought, will I be taken in by a beggar, pleading hunger and poverty.

Yet a few years later I was taken for a ride by what I thought was a poor, outcast soul. We were on holiday in Ireland, in the country, in a place called Kilkenny, visiting my sister-in-law, who was married to a farmer there. One evening as we walked through the country lanes with Tommy Tynan, my brother-in-law, going to visit a relative, out of the woods close to the roadside suddenly stepped what I took to be a real tramp. He looked as if he had been sleeping rough and needed a good wash and his clothes were well worn. He was wearing a heavy coat, with a crushed hat down one side of his head. My brother-in-law stopped to talk to him and as they were speaking, he looked me and my wife up and down. From all appearances, to me he was a down and out old tramp. I pitied him, thinking he did not have two pennies to rub together. I took 25p out of my pocket and offered it to him. He hesitated and my brother-in-law slowly shook his head at me. I could not understand why. I moved close to the man and said, 'Well, have a pint of Guinness on me.' The man still hesitated to accept my offer. I felt puzzled at his refusal to accept but I insisted he took it from me. My brother-in-law was grinning all over his face and looking me straight in the eye and shaking his head. At last the tramp accepted and thanked me, and walked away down the country lane. When he was out of earshot, Tommy asked me, bursting out laughing, 'Do you know who that was?' 'Yes,' I said, 'it was a poor man. I feel sorry for him.' 'Well,' he said, 'that man is one of the richest farmers in the country; he owns three farms round here. Tonight it will be the joke in every pub, that you gave him money for a drink.' I could not believe my ears at the story he unfolded, and sure enough when Tommy visited a pub next day, he was asked who were the rich visitors he had staying with him, who gave money to rich Farmer Murphy.

Which goes to prove one cannot judge a fellow man by his looks.

Chapter 16

In 1971, Tom Steel, the author of *The Life and Death of St Kilda*, phoned me for an interview, informing me that he was making a film of the island and would like some information about my life there. I agreed to the interview and a few days later, to my surprise, he came with his crew and television cameras and set them up in my home. Tom Steel interviewed me while his crew filmed it. A remark I made in my sitting room, 'It was a far better place', became the title of the programme. It was the first time I had ever sat in front of a television camera and it was quite an ordeal. I am very glad to have contributed a small part in the film, which was a great success in this country and in Australia where it was also shown. His book gave an insight into the life of the island long before I was born and contains many picturesque pictures of the natives and island.

Now that I am retired I have time to reflect on my past life, on the many kinds of jobs I have been employed in since I left my native Hirta and to be thankful to my Creator for His goodness to me throughout my life; for good health, an excellent wife and a happy family; to have been able to give them an opportunity and start in life which I did not have at their age. I trust they will be proud of their ancestry on both sides of the family and know that all men are equal in the sight of God. Riches and wealth, or an exciting life, was never my ambition; for by nature I love all that is natural: the hills and glens, the country and sea. As each day passes, I still traverse in dreams of my native home its shores, its caves and the way of life that once was, and wish I could return and spend a few more years in the quiet solitude of its embrace, away from the turmoil of city life, but I seem to live in memories.

Since I started to write this 'Episode of my Life', I regret I have been informed of the death of the last of the native-born Fergusons of Hirta, Neil Ferguson junior, of Kincardine, Fife. He was the last and eldest son of Neil Ferguson, sub-postmaster, and Annie Ferguson, my aunt. At Christmas he was knocked down by a car at night and sustained severe injuries from which he never fully recovered. His younger brother, Donald John, died a few years ago on the island of Arran, and his brother John, who lived in East Kilbride, also died about five years ago. Now there is only one descendant of the family alive, Neil Ferguson, son of John, living in East Kilbride.

I also received a welcome phone call lately, from a first cousin of mine, named Norman John Gillies. I have not met him since he was a boy of two years old in 1929. He informed me he was just back from a trip to St Kilda and while there he met my nephew, Andrew MacDonald, my brother's son from Stornoway. Norman John is a son of John Gillies and Mary MacQueen, my aunt. He is called after two of my uncles who were drowned at the island of Dun before I was born.

For my family tree certificate, going back to 1753, I am grateful to a Mr Gavin Ferguson, 9 Cavendish Square, London W1, who became a good friend some years back and is most interested in the island's history and its people. He has no connection to the island or the Fergusons who lived there, although he is very interested in the Clan Ferguson and he visited the island a few years back. He has gone to great trouble to get the record right regarding the past history and the descendants of the families who lived on the island. Apart from being a great dental surgeon, he is also a great historian, and travels a lot about the Western Isles and Scotland.

If I was asked, 'What have I learned from life?' I would say, 'It is a man's greed, covetousness and power to achieve his own ends, whatever the consequences to his fellow men. He is one of

God's most intelligent creatures and sometimes stoops below the animal level, to acquire and feed his lust within.'

One has only to look at his daily paper or watch the media of television every day and 'Man's inhumanity to man' stares you in the face; killings, murder, rape and crime till one feels sick to the bottom of one's soul. While there is evil in the world, there must also be goodness; yet goodness seems to take a back seat, while evil takes the front seat. It would be a great tonic to the human race, if the seats were reversed; then life would seem so much more worth living.

If I was asked who my favourite politician was at the present time, I would put Mr Enoch Powell MP in the front seat. I feel he can see into the future much more than any other. I once met him in Grosvenor House, where he was attending a cocktail party. He came into my service and said, 'Valet, is there a toilet on the floor?' 'Yes, Mr Powell,' I said, 'Follow me down the corridor.' I pointed it out to him and said, 'It's the staff toilet.' His reply was, 'It's good enough for me.' That remark impressed me, for he was not a man too proud to sit on the same 'throne' as the ordinary, working man. I stood guard outside till he came out, to prevent anyone entering his privacy. He came out, nodded and thanked me. I wonder how many of lower rank would have done the same.

Again, if I was asked who the nicest lady I ever met was (apart from my wife, of course) it would be very difficult to answer. But I think it would be a Lady I worked for when I was a footman in private service before the war: Lady Parson of Ford Bank and Carsekiey House, Southend, Kintyre. She was kind and sincere.

But the most unladylike woman was an American guest I met in Grosvenor House, shortly before I retired. Her name I shall not mention. One evening while I was on duty, a light came on in my service, indicating someone wanted my services. It was on the fifth floor and I worked from the fourth floor. I went up and noticed it was Room 514. I knocked on the door; it opened and standing there was a young woman of about twenty-five years.

She stood there wearing nothing but a very small pair of briefs. She handed me her dress and very sarcastically said, 'Press. I want it in twenty minutes.' I did not like her abrupt manner. I said, 'You will have to wait, I have two other ladies' dresses to press before I can do yours.' She went mad. 'You, Buster,' she shouted at the top of her voice at me, 'I want it in twenty minutes and not any longer.' I replied, 'I am sorry, you just have to wait your turn.' Now she was really on her high horse. 'How dare you, Buster,' she shouted at me; with that I walked away. She still shouted after me: 'You, Buster, I will have you out of here, come back here!' I carried on walking away and she carried on shouting. I got back in my service to finish the other dresses. About fifteen minutes later she marched in and said, 'Are you the chap I gave my dress to?' I said, 'Yes, I am the man.' She turned on me, wagging her finger: 'You, Buster, I am going downstairs and I am going to see you are out of here.' 'Oh,' I said, 'just get out of here and don't ever wag your finger in my face again. You can go down and make as much fuss as you wish about me, I could not care less.' She backed out of the service still shouting abuse at me. Shortly afterwards the phone rang; it was the duty manager. He asked, 'Did you go to Room 514?' I said, 'Yes.' He asked, 'What happened? She came down here really mad at you.' I explained what had happened. 'Well, for goodness sake, don't go near her again, she is wild.' I said, 'Forget it, Sir, she will calm down.' When I went back to her apartment, she was not in, so I hung it up and I never saw the lady again.

Now I sit back in my retirement and leisure hours, remembering happy, and some not so happy, days gone by.

Lasting memories on St Kilda – Malcolm (Calum) MacDonald 1908–1979, Marie Doyle 1925–2010, Finlay John MacDonald 1906–1989 (Alasdair MacEachen)